MATTHEW ARNOLD

MATTHEW ARNOLD

By

CARLETON STANLEY

President, Dalhousie University

TORONTO
THE UNIVERSITY OF TORONTO PRESS
1938

First Published, October, 1938
Reprinted, April, 1939

London:
HUMPHREY MILFORD
Oxford University Press

United States:
UNIVERSITY OF CHICAGO PRESS
Chicago, Ill.

COPYRIGHT, CANADA, 1938
PRINTED IN CANADA
Reprinted in 2018
ISBN 978-1-4875-7316-4 (paper)

W. J. A.

SOCERO, VEL ETIAM PATRI,

UNI

SAGACISSIMO

GENEROSISSIMO

HUMANISSIMO,

HAEC DEDICO.

C. S.

THE ALEXANDER LECTURES IN ENGLISH
AT
THE UNIVERSITY OF TORONTO
1938

THE ALEXANDER LECTURESHIP

THE Alexander Lectureship was founded in honour of Professor W. J. Alexander, Head of the Department of English Literature in University College from 1889 to 1926. The funds necessary for the purpose were collected by a large number of the old students and friends of Professor Alexander immediately after his retirement. The object of the lectureship is to bring to the University each year a distinguished critic, man of letters, or university professor, usually from another country, who will give a course of from three to six lectures on some subject related to English Literature. The lectures are published either by the lecturer himself or by the University of Toronto Press. The list of Alexander lecturers since 1929 is as follows: Professor Cazamian of the Sorbonne, Professor Garrod of Oxford, Professor Babbitt of Harvard, Sir William Craigie of Chicago, Professor Grierson of Edinburgh, Professor Sedgewick of British Columbia, Professor Stoll of Minnesota, Professor Snyder of Northwestern, Professor Nichol Smith of Oxford, and President Carleton Stanley of Dalhousie.

PREFACE

I TAKE this opportunity to thank my old friend and teacher, Principal Malcolm W. Wallace, and his colleagues on the English staff, for their invitation to deliver these lectures.* I am grateful also for the very friendly encouragement which they and others, notably my schoolmaster, F. C. Colbeck, and my Greek professor, J. C. Robertson, gave me while they were being delivered. The hospitality of the University was boundless, and yet not irksome.

It delighted me to have in my audience a member of the University who remembered Matthew Arnold being brought there by his friend, Goldwin Smith, also a lady who had heard Arnold give his lecture, *Numbers*, in Montreal.

C. S.

July, 1938.

*Delivered January 31 to February 4, 1938.

CONTENTS

		PAGE
Chapter I.	Introduction	13
Chapter II.	Arnold's Poetry	41
Chapter III.	Arnold's Poetry (*continued*)	71
Chapter IV.	Arnold the Critic and Prose Writer	99
Chapter V.	Arnold the Critic and Prose Writer (*continued*)	122
Index		157

I

INTRODUCTION

MATTHEW ARNOLD is undoubtedly in poetry, and I believe also in some of his prose, a classic: that is to say he has succeeded in addressing himself to all times. And yet, if ever an author, in poetry or prose, addressed himself to his own day and generation, on the surrounding scene, it was he. Further, from the first he was intensely conscious of the changes in thought and outlook that his times were bringing with them; hardly less conscious of the change which his father and other forceful men had wrought during his boyhood, and the bent which forcible men of the next generation might still give the seemingly omnipotent stream of events. It is of considerable importance, therefore, to seize with what clearness is possible to us the general character of Matthew Arnold's age, 1822-88; not to become lost in names and details, and not to see some of the drifts and tendencies and forces to the exclusion of others; for except in one important respect he is intimately connected with all the movements.

In some respects the period was like our own. Both Europe and America were in a flux: in politics, in social questions of all sorts, in religious belief and unbelief, in the advance of scientific principles and theories, and also in their application. Like our own period, it was one of recovery from a world-shaking war, not so truly a world-war as the last, but yet a war which engaged most of Europe for a quarter century, and other parts of the world at intervals. On the surface Britain seemed to recover more rapidly than some other countries, but even in Britain the prolonged external struggle had postponed a consideration of pressing political, social, and educational problems at home, so that recovery applied unequally to different strata in society. As is usual also, the liberty of the individual had been curtailed in the long struggle and afterwards. Again, there were epidemics of diseases, completely baffling to the medical profession.[1]

In other respects the general situation was very different. Much of the world was unexplored. Population, despite epidemics, was increasing. Until late in Arnold's life there was no Italy, and no Germany, in our sense of the words. France was still an object of suspicion to the politicians and newspapers; only some, better informed, feared Russia, and indeed the map which shows the territorial aggrandizement of Russia during the nineteenth century is the most striking of all historical maps. It is perhaps an unanswerable

---

[1] Is bewilderment to be seen in the name *Asiatic cholera*, as in the name *Spanish influenza?*

question whether the new physics and astronomy of our day have caused so great an adjustment of the human mind as the geology and biology of Arnold's day. At least we have had the earlier example to brace and steady us.

At any rate, if we reflect a moment on some of the things here outlined, we can see that the Victorian Age in England is as unlike what the half-educated person of our day means by the phrase as can well be imagined. Certainly it was not an age of torpor and complacency, and though it may be called a fairly barren time in some of the arts, architecture and painting and the domestic arts, some more and some less, it was still an age fertile of poetry and imaginative prose, and a great new era in science. It would seem that biology is the least congenial of sciences to the human mind. It was the first of the sciences to disappear in the disintegration of Hellenic civilization; it became extinct with Theophrastus early in the third century B.C.; it was the last of the sciences to reappear among West Europeans. For some hundreds of years, Europeans had been recovering and even extending the mathematics and the mathematical sciences which the Greeks had carried to such a pitch of perfection. But in many respects West Europeans did not catch up with Greek biology until the late nineteenth century. Arnold's contemporaries in England had much to do with it.

He, himself, was all but blind on this side. But with most other human activities he himself had to do, not officially nor as a great public figure; indeed, until his later life, he was not much in the public eye. He never attained popularity as Tennyson did, nor even notoriety, as half a dozen other contemporaries did. He might be called, rather, the Socrates of his age; and indeed like Socrates, he was much ahead of his time. But if we call him that we must limit the scope of the phrase to the readers of reviews: he did not talk to the public on the street corner.

It was Arnold's wish that no biography of him be written. We still have none, and his works have long been out of print. But there will presently be materials for a biography, and I shall be surprised if a publisher does not soon bring out a collected edition of his works, there being so many signs of a revival of interest. I give but two examples: one a solid literary scholar, and another whom I hardly know how to characterize, beyond saying that he has a great vogue with the demi-literate. In 1932, Sir Edmund Chambers, whom all students of English literature knew so long as E. K. Chambers, said in a lecture on Arnold's poetry to the British Academy: "One may fairly maintain that the proportion of work which endures is greater in the case of Matthew Arnold than in that of any of his six greatest contemporaries." (The expression is cryptic on one side, but the meaning is plain so far as Arnold is concerned.) A year later, T. S. Eliot, Professor of Poetry in Harvard University, gave a lecture on Arnold as poet and critic. Dismissing *The Forsaken Merman* as a "charade"; without any allusion to *Thyrsis* or to many of the other finest poems; calling him a petulant and arrogant critic; he makes this as his most general observation about Arnold: "Even if the delight we get from Arnold's writings, prose and verse, be moderate, yet he is in some respects the most satisfactory man of letters of his age." On Sir Edmund Chambers's comment I make two observations: first, that it coincides closely in spirit with what George Eliot said of Matthew Arnold in his lifetime; second, that, having been a lover of some of Arnold's poems since boyhood, and of more and more of them as reading and experience grew, I find more and more that those who are well-read in European literature, ancient and modern, give him high place. As for T. S. Eliot, one might say that even those who seem most incapable of knowing or appreciating anything have somehow come to suspect that Matthew Arnold is wearing better than most of his contemporaries.

Certain facts: the absence of a biography, the

difficulty in dating his poems, the unrepresentative selection of his work in anthologies, his connection with the Oxford of Newman, and with Clough, who left Oxford out of religious difficulties—all these things have caused too much attention to be given to Arnold's interest in religion, and far too little attention to be given to his interest in social and political questions. The first poems, and the first private letters, do not show preoccupation with religious difficulties, but they do show an immense preoccupation with revolution in Europe, and poverty and misery at home. Even in his boyish poem, *Alaric at Rome*, there is a hint of this. The *Sonnets to a Friend*, printed when he was twenty-six, are worth study in this respect. Even if we did not know that the friend was Clough, a most peculiarly intimate and family friend, the sonnets as they stand are obviously an unburdening of soul. True, one of the sonnets is entitled *Religious Isolation*, but clearly it is the friend, not Arnold, who has religious difficulties. His own preoccupation, while he claims "in these bad days" to "prop" himself with Homer, Epictetus, and above all Sophocles, breaks through again and again, in these sonnets and in other poems of the same period, in such phrases as:

> thoughts, not idle, while before me flow
> The armies of the homeless and unfed.

He bemoans the "avarice and envy" of men,

INTRODUCTION 19

Britain's intentness on increasing commerce, and so forth.

These early poems were written by a fairly fortunate young man, considered by his family and intimate friends to have no great seriousness, and indeed to have somewhat affected manners and to indulge in foppish attire. This may have been a self-imposed screen, and of a youthful kind; but at no time in his life did Arnold allow inner agitations to disturb his outer man. His real self, and much of his future, is to be found in these early poems, written in the "terrible forties", to use the phrase of the historian:

> thoughts, not idle, while before me flow
> The armies of the homeless and unfed.

Besides the miserable masses in England itself there were the outpourings of the Irish proletariat. Canada did not receive all of them. In the two years previous to July, 1847, 300,000 absolutely destitute Irish had landed in Liverpool. One quarter stayed there, dying like flies, and carrying death to others. The rest drifted inland. A report of 1847[2] reveals fifty to sixty of these waifs living in tenements of three to four rooms. Sometimes forty or more would be found sleeping in a cellar. The same authority says that a few years later gangs of Irish were drafted in by East Anglian

---

[2]Quoted by Professor J. A. Clapham, in his chapter "Work and Wages", *Early Victorian England*, ed. G. M. Young, Oxford Press, 1934.

farmers "to break the greatest, the only great, agricultural labourers' strike of the century". In the year before Arnold published these sonnets, the year when political revolutions were so unsuccessful on the continent, Chartism collapsed in England. Ten years earlier the Chartists had presented their first petition to Parliament. I quote it in part:

> We, your petitioners, dwell in a land whose merchants are noted for their enterprise, whose manufacturers are very skilful, and whose workmen are proverbial for their industry. The land itself is goodly, the soil rich and temperature wholesome. It is abundantly furnished with arteries for commerce, it has numerous and convenient harbors; in facility of internal communication it exceeds all others. For three and twenty years it has enjoyed profound peace. Yet with all these elements of national prosperity, and with every disposition and capacity to take advantage of them, we find ourselves overwhelmed with public and private suffering. Our workmen are starving, capital brings no profit and labor no remuneration. . . . We have searched diligently to find the causes of a distress so sore and so long continued. We can discover none in Nature or Providence.

One may read accounts of children of seven or less working in mills from 5 a.m. to 9 p.m., beaten when they fell asleep. Instead of speculating whether this sort of thing was general or sporadic, it is better to place oneself in the hands of an acknowledged authority, and a judicious critic. Professor J. A. Clapham (*op. cit.*) says:

> Mere babies of three or four were put to cottage lace-making and straw-plaiting in the 'sixties. . . . Children were regularly sent to learn how to seam knitted gloves at five years old, sometimes at three and a-half. . . . After long discussion . . . and a fierce agitation in the north . . . the State had started a comprehensive system for the regulation of the labour of children and "young persons" in textile factories in 1833. It came fully into force in 1836, and was on its trial during the next ten years. The factory workers and their allies, who had aimed at regulation of the whole industry by means of a Ten Hours' Bill, not merely at regulation of youthful and child labour, considered themselves betrayed. Their employers, now well represented in Parliament, especially after the arrival of Cobden at Westminster in 1841, believed themselves unjustly victimised. . . . The dominant employers' view, which Bright shared with Cobden, was that State "interference" must be, in some undetermined economic-political sense, wrong; and that, in any event, selective interference was most demonstrably unjust. . . .
>
> The factories had been regulated mainly because they were new and conspicuous, and because, in early days, men connected with them—the elder Peel and Robert Owen—had demanded regulation. Mines went downwards—the miners had always been something of a race apart—and no mine-owner had ever taken up their cause before the world. So the report of half-naked women underground, girls crawling as draught-animals in the dirt of narrow workings, and

little boys sitting solitary, opening and shutting ventilation doors in gross darkness, all day long where there was no day—these things disgusted even people usually apathetic. The worst things were far from universal. . . . Parliament at once (1842), driven on by Lord Ashley's prompt use of the general disgust, ordered the women out of the pits; said that boys were not to go down them under the age of ten. . . . The new law took some years to get into full operation. . . .

With child labour outside the textile factories and mines the early Victorian Parliament never dealt systematically. The report of 1843, which followed that on the mines, showed that it existed everywhere, and was abused in all kinds of ways. Reports of 1863-6 said very much the same. . . . Taking the country as a whole, regular work generally began between the ages of seven and eight. . . .

Only a portion of the children in England went to school. R. H. Mottram[3] quotes from reports on Bristol and Leeds made in the 'thirties: "Of 6,000 children (in Bristol) 2,500 escaped school." He says that in Leeds, which he calls more typical, "rudimentary schools provided for 7,000 children; the Sunday schools took in 11,000; 15,000 went altogether untaught". But when it is said that so and so many children of any community went to school, it should be remembered that the average school life of these fortunate ones was short.

---

[3] *Early Victorian England*, chap. iii.

INTRODUCTION

G. M. Young[4] guesses that it "was perhaps two years, perhaps eighteen months". He cites an investigation in Salford, where it was found that less than half of those at school were taught to read or write. Indeed many of the alleged "teachers" could not sign their own names, for in the census of 1851 more than two per cent of the private schoolmasters and mistresses signed their returns with a mark.[5] Many even of those who had learned to read, write, and cipher, when young children, soon forgot these accomplishments in the grinding toil which succeeded. As against this we can imagine that many other persons, like Cobbett, learned to read when adult.

The more advanced medical authorities of a slightly later period, notably Dr. Snow on *Asiatic Cholera*,[6] and Dr. Budd on *Typhoid Fever*,[7] give a cross-section of the life of this period which cannot be overlooked. There were terrible epidemics of cholera in 1832, 1848, and 1853. In the last year, 1853, nearly two per cent of the population died of cholera in Newcastle, in nine weeks. And Newcastle was a markedly enlightened place, according to contemporary accounts. In each year, 1832 and 1848, Dumfries lost over three per cent of its population through the same disease. In mines, and in such institutions as orphanages, the disease

---
[4]"Portrait of an Age" in *Early Victorian England*.
[5]See *Early Victorian England*, vol. II, p. 3.
[6]John Snow, M.D., *On the Mode of Communication of Cholera*, 1855.
[7]William Budd, M.D., F.R.S., *Typhoid Fever*, 1873.

would wipe out nearly fifteen per cent of the population in a short period. As late as 1859, ten per cent of the population in the country places of Wiltshire and Wales were suffering with typhoid. In London, of course, both diseases wrought fearful havoc, and the private companies supplying water showed the most callous indifference to advanced medical opinion on the communication of these diseases.

It seems to be idle to lament that Matthew Arnold forsook poetry for prose, and "literature" for political and religious writing. What sort of vacuum is "literature" supposed to be? Idle also to wish that he had lived in another age, or been another person. Matthew Arnold as he was, Matthew Arnold born in England in 1822, did not divide experience into sealed compartments such as poetry, criticism, literature, politics, religion. Glance at his early poems; aside from the prize poems, the sonnet on Shakespeare, dated 1844, is the earliest extant to which we can assign a certain date. Is it not criticism? We may wish, if we choose, but again it is an idle wish, that Arnold had found an easier occupation than that of school inspector. But had it been so he would not have been the well-informed person he was. His friend, J. A. Froude, wrote, on reading Arnold's first published poems that "Matt" knew the seamy side of life only from books. This was perhaps an exaggeration even at that period, for

INTRODUCTION 25

no man with his eyes open, certainly no man with Arnold's human sympathy and his hatred of ugliness, could live in England through the 'forties and fail to know the seamy side of life. But when, two years later, he became school inspector and also worked for his father-in-law, Judge Wightman, and went up and down England, on circuit and visiting schools, staying at commercial hotels, Arnold had unrivalled opportunities for studying the seamy side. It is a mistake to represent Arnold as "taking up" theology late in life and as an intruder in that field. Some of his own remarks, in his prefaces, might seem to bear out the statement that he turned from one thing to another. Arnold's *Letters* tell another story, and his complete journal would probably reveal him a life-long student of theology, though an *amateur* in this as in other things.

In view of Arnold's life-long reserve, and knowing as we do that he remained an enigma to his family and intimate friends, we should not be too precise as to his personality. But one thing, apparent on the outside, and explaining his versatile industry, is worth noting. Like his father he was a most energetic person. Writing to his mother of Ely and Peterborough Cathedrals in 1861, he recalls the last time he saw them; his father on that expedition had carried him pick-a-back to the top of Peterborough Cathedral. He himself is always hurrying to catch trains or ships. In the same year he tells of his wife's alarm because they and three of their children were still on the landing stage at Portsmouth when the Ryde steamer began to move. On the return journey his wife almost missed the same steamer. His correspondence, in hundreds of places, describes a day which most strong men would have considered overfilled. But these were his normal days. At the age of forty-five he is writing to his brother, in the early dawn, at Cambridge. With no complaint he mentions that he will inspect school that day, travel all night (not in a sleeper!), reach home in London at five next morning, and begin his day's work four hours later. (At this time he was preparing an important collection of poems for the publisher.) He hopes to have a holiday with his brother later, in Scotland, "but it will depend on money, the children and other things". He had recently failed in applications for two positions, one of which would have increased his salary, the other of which would have given him an easier life. He had now six children, the eldest a hopeless invalid. To return to the letter: it is a long one, and is brought abruptly to an end, so that he can dress, breakfast, and catch a train. We learn from another letter of October this year, that he did not have his holiday: his wife had been very ill, and had stayed with her

INTRODUCTION

mother during a long convalescence; he himself had been house-hunting for his enlarged family, and had had only a couple of days' shooting near London. He was addicted to physical exercise; he was an ardent fly-fisherman from youth to age, and pursued that pastime when too ill to do other things. Clough complained that he went long distances to fish when he should have been working for his final Oxford examination. He always had a rod with him on his holidays. Like most real pedestrians he preferred walking in hilly or mountainous country, and according to his own account he did not like sea-level. He skated whenever he could, even after dark. At thirty-seven he joined the militia in London, but as he could drill only from 7 to 9 p.m. it meant that he missed his dinner twice a week. This latter he thought an advantage, and the drill was "so good for the muscles". His inspectoral duties seem frequently to have allowed no intermission for lunch. Despite his abstemiousness and regular exercise he seems never to have enjoyed very good health. He was subject to coughs and colds, headaches, lumbago, and frequent toothache, though he always attributes these ailments to low spirits, and sometimes to idleness, especially idleness from poetic composition. Even towards the end, when he had had several heart attacks, he could not resist tennis.

All this clearly indicates driving physical energy. His father had been called "bustling". A physician of to-day would most probably have discovered high blood-pressure in both father and son. The letters indicate, as well as the poems, an alternate love for society and an aversion from it. From both sources, and not least from the private note-book, we see a natural tendency to fits of depression, and a schooled resolve to rise above them.

We have seen that religious questions appeared to Arnold as a part of the whole social complex, and that at the outset he was more troubled by the squalor and ugliness, the injustice and misery of life, than by what he believed or how that belief was expressed. The "Oxford Movement", a contrast with his own upbringing, must, one would have thought, have set him thinking about religious questions. It does not appear to have done so at an early period. What struck him first, apparently, was the even greater contrast between Christianity as he had been taught it, and the Christianity he saw all round him. Much as he loved the Established Church for the beauty of its ritual and the beauty of its churches, the heavy unintelligence of some of its clergy moved him to satire. There is an eloquent paragraph in an early letter to Clough on that subject. When he began to live among Dissenters, who

INTRODUCTION 29

boldly laid claim to a purer form of Christian faith, his mirth was stirred by their quaint eccentricities; he was appalled by the ugliness of their chapels, the muddy bathos of their hymns, and their seeming determination to have schools whose light should be as darkness. Most of his ideas about contemporary Dissenters were valid. But some aspects of the matter were hidden from him, and this causes me to glance at some of Matthew Arnold's limitations.

Quick as he was with historical analogies, he lacked any deep and abiding historic sense. I know that this will not be readily admitted by Arnold's admirers, and I shall return to the subject again. Here I shall deal with it sufficiently to illustrate developments among the Dissenters which he missed. About some matters, but not many, he had that historic insight into contemporary events which distinguishes the commentary made on French politics by Walter Bagehot, an insight given only to few men in any generation. In the later 'thirties and early 'forties—the "most terrible period in modern England", it has been called—the hated Dissenters were here and there, quite of their own effort, establishing great movements. The Wesleyans had for the most part prospered, become intent on money-making, and grown conservative; but the uglier Chapels, in the ugliest parts of industrial England, were behind the Rochdale "cooperatives", behind the "thrift societies", behind the free library movements; it was also among them that the efforts of Joseph Livesay and the "Lancashire teetotallers" were most effective. They may have had little sweetness, but they had seen a light not yet apparent to others.

Another limitation was more serious. Though he often uses the word science, and though, like so many of his contemporaries, he began in late life to dabble in botany, Arnold had no insight whatever into science, and consequently missed the significance, in large part, of the most striking characteristic of his age. This is not to say that he missed the general effect of the contemporary movement. In this respect it might be instructive to survey his life and the life of Tyndall side by side. They were almost exactly contemporaries (1822-88; 1820-93). Both have long been comparatively neglected, and their works are hard to find in either libraries or book-shops. Tyndall is much the slighter figure, yet, like Arnold, he partly shaped the time. Self-taught until the age of twenty-eight, he was then able to spend three years at the University of Marburg. His teaching there was wholly scientific, yet I think we can see from his once famous address to the British Association in Belfast, 1874, that he appreciated poetry and imagination more than Arnold appreciated science.[8]

And yet it is easily possible to push these arguments too far. Arnold had at once a readiness of human sympathy, and a sheer critical power that enabled him to lay a quick finger on some of the symptoms of his period, and allowed him to predict the future, in some phases, as did few men of his time. Much might be made of his inability to do anything with mathematics at Oxford, and his consequent inability to understand science. As against that it should be remembered that with one night's coaching he swept the logic examination. No man of his time was quicker to pierce the illogic of an argument, or a position, whether in politics, social questions, theology, or rational statement. In this respect Ruskin, Macaulay, Carlyle, Newman, Darwin are babes beside him. I think it was his sympathy and humanity, added to sufficient historical knowledge, that made him see so clearly into the Irish question, a question that has always been the cruellest test for the intelligence of Englishmen. But it was sheer sagacity that made him understand the fundamental im-

---

[8] In 1866 Arnold began to speak of Tyndall's views on education with great respect, but hearing him lecture two years later, he was disappointed. Arnold was on a friendlier footing with Huxley; both had a real turn for logic, and a somewhat similar vein of humour.

portance of England's undertaking national education; that made him distrust the materialism of the United States, and predict that if unchecked it would swamp Europe as well; and that, above all, enabled him to see that the idolatry of ugliness, or even the toleration of ugliness, can destroy a civilization. It is perhaps chiefly this last part of Arnold's genius that we have not overtaken to-day. We should all admit, at least I hope we should, that he was right about Ireland, right about English schools, right about the future of the United States and its menace to Europe; but as for his most insistent teaching, that to tolerate ugliness in thought or speech or act harms an individual and destroys society, this seems, to many of Arnold's admirers even, an extreme aestheticism, and to the great majority either an unimportant doctrine or sheer folly. Some affect to see in it a sort of prudery; they connect it with his definition of poetry, which definition they utterly condemn, as a criticism of life. Others, remembering perhaps what they have read in text-books, or truncated translations of Plato, condemn Arnold and Plato together. These writers do not understand that here, Matthew Arnold, who missed the scientific legacy of Greece, is straight in line with all the rest of its immense legacy: its worship of beauty in Nature, and beauty in humanity, its austere subordination of part to whole, its dread of irrelevance, disproportion, exaggeration, and its positive loathing of the ugly. And by *ugly* the most civilized of the Greeks meant a number of things which we should hardly dream of calling ugly; such as a mere lack of simplicity in music or speech, or awkwardness in bearing, an eccentricity of dress, a parade of immorality. Now it is sometimes suggested that such doctrines as these are to be found only in Plato, and that Plato was a Puritan, and to that extent un-Greek. A scholar, of course, knows better; he has read dozens of other Greek authors besides Plato, and has seen the doctrine exemplified in thousands of Greek works of art, from coins to temples, from kitchen utensils to public statues. And if he has made some attempt to understand European development he knows that by this doctrine, as well as by their mathematics, physics, astronomy, biology, and political thought, the Greeks have potently shaped the world; he knows too that when Europeans have either flouted or forgotten this doctrine, for example Rubens and Teniers[9] in art, Machiavelli in politics, the Puritans in religion, mill-owners in architecture, they have dealt a blow to themselves and their posterity.

Matthew Arnold, then, is not merely a "great Victorian", whether we use that phrase in praise or blame. He was a great poet in an age of poetry, but notwithstanding his failure to under-

---

[9] I refer to "Kermesse" pictures of Teniers, the elder.

stand it fully as an age of science, he was unrivalled in his powers of criticizing his time, and in many respects our time. Nor has his mantle fallen on any successor. He looks before and after with more certainty and more universality than is nowadays generally admitted. He is not to be dismissed with the phrases that were levelled at him in his own time: a poet who had missed his calling by becoming a school inspector; a literary gentleman who perversely dabbled in politics and religion; an elegant Jeremiah who had lost himself in the world of reality. These and other caricaturing phrases show not merely his versatility: they show in how many ways his generation needed him. The fact that they are still repeated indicates how much we still have to do for ourselves.

At this point it will appear, on first thoughts, that I begin to digress. But the relevance of what I say in the next few pages will be seen in the later lectures. It was suggested to me, at the beginning, that I take as my subject for these lectures the influence of Greek poetry and thought on English poetry. A fascinating subject truly, but far too vast for a single series of lectures, even if it were within my powers. Greek poetry is a vast field: only those who have strayed and studied in it, not a brief while, but most of a lifetime, have the faintest idea of its extent, its multitudinous variety, and its profound and endlessly suggestive representation of human experience. Homer is a world in himself. It was an Englishman who said in the last century: "A man who has never read Homer is like a man who has never seen the ocean; there is a great experience he has missed." And Homer, from Milton to the present, has influenced our poets great and small. To be sure, some of our English poets, like other European poets, have assimilated Homer less thoroughly than others. What puts one off, frequently, in reading Vergil, is the sense that he is a derivative in an awkward way. Or, to change the metaphor, he takes an Homeric framework, of which the reader who knows Homer is intensely aware; he has not knocked down the scaffolding round his own building. In a similar way, Dante takes a Vergilian framework, though Dante is more purely himself than is Vergil. It may be Milton's steeping and drenching in Hebraic literature that saves him partly from any artificial imitation of Homer. More probably Arnold was right in ascribing Milton's complete assimilation of Homer to his own nobility of nature. Certain it is that despite Homer's comparative simplicity, or rather artlessness, and Milton's much more obvious art, there is a ring of grandeur in Milton, even in his most obvious phrase, that is on Homer's heights and yet characteristically Miltonic. Like

Aeschylus among the later Greeks, Milton is big enough, grand enough, to make Homer part of himself. Akin to this grandeur of utterance is another feature in Homer which I believe Arnold nowhere notices, the feeling a reader has of sweeping through a spacious universe as one reads. The supreme example of this in Homer's long chain of successors is Lucretius; indeed, in this respect Lucretius out-Homer's Homer. When Vergil attempts it in the sixth *Aeneid*, the result is a mere misty obfuscation, the oppression of being lost in a thick forest at night—a feature in Vergil which Dante seems to have admired. Now this Homeric sweep is often caught in Milton, as often in descriptions of the bright Empyrean as of the glooms of Hell. One sees it magnificently done in the second half of Book II and throughout Book III of *Paradise Lost*. *Balder Dead* fails, as Vergil fails, in this respect.

But it is not right to mention *Balder Dead*, even in passing, without speaking of *Sohrab and Rustum*. I do so briefly by instituting another comparison. Tennyson's imitations of Homer are intensely artificial and Vergilian always. The opening of *Morte d'Arthur*, for example, once so much admired:

> So all day long the noise of battle rolled
> Among the mountains by the winter sea;

is an echo of the opening of the sixth *Iliad*:

Τρώων δ' οἰώθη καὶ Ἀχαιῶν φύλοπις αἰνή,
πολλὰ δ' ἄρ' ἔνθα καὶ ἔνθ ἴθυσε μάχη πεδίοιο,
ἀλλήλων ἰθυνομένων χαλκήρεα δοῦρα,
μεσσηγὺς Σιμόεντος ἰδὲ Ξάνθοιο ῥοάων.

How faint, how dragging, and mouthing, and feminine, is Tennyson compared with his original! As we know from a letter to Clough, readers of *Sohrab and Rustum* charged Arnold with imitating *Morte d'Arthur*. Arnold confessed that unconsciously he might have, but he rather thought that those who saw a resemblance did so because both Tennyson and he had been aware of Homer, and he thought he had been aware of him to better purpose. I think this undeniably true.

So far have we gone in speaking of only Homer among the Greeks, and in giving only a few examples of his influence! There is Plato, a poet if ever there was one, though he wrote almost entirely in prose; Plato, an empire in himself, and wielding a sovereign influence on our poetry from Spenser's time to the present day. Here, once more, the influence has been at times closely and deeply assimilated, as by Shelley, or imitated from afar and without much penetration, as by Spenser.

The influence of Attic tragedy, both direct and indirect, on English poetry is well nigh incalculable; a voluminous work might be written on it. It affected our drama even through the mediaeval religious drama. In the very year when

an English scholar was denying this—1890—
Krumbacher was tracing the effect of Euripides'
Bacchae on Christian work of the eleventh and
twelfth centuries. Our Elizabethan tragedy took
a line of its own, as is well known. It is not
Attic. Once, and once only, an English poet
completely caught in dramatic work the spirit of
Attic tragedy, and here again Milton completely
assimilated his models. Swinburne and Browning
fail in very different ways, Shelley at times comes
nearer to it, and so does Thomas Hardy. Of
Arnold's attempts at Greek tragedy, more later.
But the direct influences of Attic tragic writers on
English poetry are to be seen, I think, not in the
writers of tragedy.

Knowing then the vastness of the subject
suggested, and aware of the discursiveness into
which it would lead a lecturer—I offer my own
remarks during the last few pages as an illustration—I suggested a compromise: the treatment
of an English author in whom the effects of Greek
literature are plainly to be seen, and also an
author of whom I had long wished to speak.

The influence of Greek poetry and thought on
Matthew Arnold, as I shall try to show in the
lectures that are to follow, is not too obvious or
obtrusive, if we are willing to leave two of his long
works out of the picture. When he laboured consciously and deliberately to represent that poetry

and thought—in *Merope* and *Balder Dead*—he failed. I will not say that too much has been made of these failures—but it has too often been assumed that he was always attempting classical exercises. It has been denied that he had any poetic inspiration at all. It is sometimes held that his subject-matter is incapable of poetic treatment, and again that he had no metrical skill, and no ear. How these writers explain away his great poetic accomplishment is hard to discover. I think him a poet highly inspired and highly gifted; there is no other way of accounting for much of his poetry. But by temper as well as training he is almost a fifth- or fourth-century Athenian set down in nineteenth-century England. That, and not merely his brooding over a lost faith, is his disequilibrium. Intensely aware of the dignity and beauty possible to human society he sees the bulk of his countrymen in a religious prison-house; great masses of the people, and legions of little children even, slaves to factories and mines, and without even a slave's security or a slave's value to an owner; and such serenity and beauty as there once had been for the more fortunate in society now rapidly being dissolved by new elements. Despite this he breathes an Attic spirit in his own work; in his poetry there is a mature wisdom appealing to the elemental and universal in man; austerely expressed, without pomp, ornament, or tinkling music; and sometimes falling into lines as perfect and flawless as anything we know; and in his best prose—as we shall see it is not his best prose that is to-day always most admired—there is an Attic subtlety of understatement and irony, and an Attic urbanity and incapacity for dullness.

II

ARNOLD'S POETRY

ARNOLD'S first volume of verse, *A Strayed Reveller and Other Poems*, appeared in February, 1849, two months after his twenty-sixth birthday. Five hundred copies were printed, and they bore as signature only the initial "A". A few close friends pierced the disguise. In our present state of knowledge it is impossible to set dates on all the poems in this edition, as indeed it is often difficult, frequently impossible, to set dates on the poems in the later editions. The author apparently never cared to take his readers into confidence in this matter. As to the poems in the first edition one can say, however, where the touch is sure and where it is not. In the poem which gave the title to the collection, the *Strayed Reveller*, we see for the most part experiment and immaturity, though it has subtleties and contains characteristic things. For example, one sees the influence of Homer, and not less the influence of Herodotus, Arnold's love of Alpine scenery; the "Chorasmian stream" looks forward to *Sohrab and Rustum*; and there is already the elegiac lament for a lost tranquillity of mind. But nothing is firmly grasped or convincingly stated.

For the most part, the sonnets in this collection

do not quite succeed. They are much quoted, for they contain great phrases, some of which have passed into the language, great lines and fine imagery. But they halt somehow, they do not flow like Wordsworth's; one has to read them carefully in certain places even to construe them; I have never been absolutely certain that I knew to a shade what the concluding lines of two of them mean—the one on Shakespeare and the one on Emerson. These are probably the earliest of the sonnets; the former was completed at least as early as 1844, and we know that Arnold was reading and talking about Emerson two years before that time. Two of these early sonnets, however, do run flowingly and are as lucid as anything in Arnold: the one beginning:

Who prop, thou ask'st, in these bad days, my mind?

and the other beginning:

God knows it, I am with you.

We pass completely from experiment and immaturity when we come to *Mycerinus*. Milton had given a hint in *Il Penseroso* of what might be done by an English poet in retelling old Greek tales. In the long line of English poets since, no one has so perfectly retold a Greek story as Arnold has done here. It is from Herodotus, that perfect teller of tales, Herodotus who for many an Englishman has been the favourite author, as he was perhaps the favourite author of Plato and

Sophocles. Though the story is from Herodotus, it is an Egyptian legend, and like a Greek, or we might say like an Englishman, Herodotus is somewhat aghast at the immorality, or, let us say, the poetic injustice of it. But Arnold, while catching the spirit of Herodotus, has perfectly assimilated his material. *Mycerinus* is an English poem, and a very beautiful and flawless one. The first part of the poem is a dramatic monologue, in a six-line stanza; the second part is descriptive in blank verse.

Saintsbury, who always called Tennyson "a great poet" and Arnold "not quite great", says of this blank verse, in a puzzled way: "it is not un-Tennysonian, and yet different from Tennyson." The truth is, I think, that it is superior to Tennyson's blank verse in its "quietness", to use the word as Arnold himself later used it when he said that *Thyrsis* was "a very quiet poem". It does not aim, as Tennyson aimed, at jewelled lines, lines which bring one to a stop, and distract us from the theme; it aims at, and secures, a total effect. It is altogether free from Tennyson's sweetishness and his unmasculinity.

Let us look now at *The Forsaken Merman*. Writing to Clough, eight days after the *Strayed Reveller and Other Poems* appeared, J. A. Froude said:

> I admire Matt—to a very great extent. Only I don't see what business he has to parade his calm-

ness and lecture us on resignation when he has never known what a storm is, and doesn't know what he has to resign himself to—I think he knows the seamy side of nature out of books.—Still I think his versifying and generally his aesthetic power is quite wonderful. . . . On the whole he shapes better than *you* I think—but you have marble to cut out and he has only clay. I do not know that I should say "only". There are some things, like the *Forsaken Merman*, that sound right out from the heart.

In the collected poems as they finally stand, *The Forsaken Merman* has immediately placed before it a strange poem called *The Neckan*. I cannot discover when this was written. It tells much the same story about a sea-king, but in a very wooden way, and the scene is the shore of the Baltic. Of course there were many Greek legends about sea-nymphs and sea-kings marrying mortals. But *The Forsaken Merman* is neither Norse, nor Greek, but straight out from the heart, as Froude said. I have quoted Froude so fully because these remarks show not only his divination, but also a trait in Arnold's character. He kept his inner thoughts and also his composing, for the most part, completely to himself. Froude was long a mentor of his, Clough very much so; but except two letters to Clough, one from the Baths of Leuk, September, 1848, and one from Thun, September, 1849, the first with a cryptic reference to a "pair of bright eyes" at the hotel at Thun, and a declaration that he wants to be done with women, and the second with a quotation from *Parting*, which was published in 1852, a quotation altogether unintelligible if taken by itself, there is as yet no account or explanation of the passionate love affair with Marguerite, or Margaret, or whatever her name was. But *The Forsaken Merman* is written out of that passion, and Froude knowing nothing of the circumstances, pierced to the secret. I shall refer later to other poems on the same subject; I am now dealing only with *The Forsaken Merman*.

Most readers of Arnold place it high among his poems, some highest of all. In a way it is a slight thing; if Arnold's definition of poetry, "a criticism of life", be strained ridiculously, as some have strained it, then *The Forsaken Merman* being a mere myth, is not poetry at all. I have admired it increasingly all my life, for I encountered it in a school reader compiled by the man in whose honour these lectures are given. I say now that I know nothing in all English poetry so flawlessly beautiful in expression. Will those who tell us that Arnold's poetry is derivative tell us whence he derived this? No, no! Froude, groping his way, unsure, contradicting himself, still, a week after the poem first appeared, put his finger directly on the matter: *The Forsaken Merman* "sounds right out from the heart". And it is one of the great things of our literature.

It is apposite to this place to deal now with the other poems which bear directly or indirectly on the "daughter of France" whom Arnold met in Switzerland in September, 1848, and again in September, 1849. We do not know whether he had seen her before that, or whether he ever saw her later. These poems were published, for the first time, some in 1849, some in 1852, some in 1853, some in 1855, and one in 1867. But we do not know, for certain, when they were written. Some other verses on the same theme, as we know from the letters to Clough, which appeared in 1932,[1] were never published at all. My belief is that except the one which first appeared in 1867, *The Terrace at Berne*, they were all written before his attachment to Miss Wightman, with whom Arnold began to correspond in 1850, and whom he married in 1851. Arnold's family long gave it out that the inspiration of these poems was sheer fancy, but no reader of them has 'ever believed that. Just as Samuel Butler, writing long before M. Legouis unearthed Wordsworth's passion for Annette Vallon, said, in his own mocking way, that the Lucy poems must have sprung from something in Wordsworth's experience, so writers about Arnold have said that the poems called *Switzerland*,

---

[1] Professor Lowry's admirable edition.

in the 1855 edition, and other poems published earlier, pointed to an early passion. Professor Lowry, who has seen the Arnold journals and other papers not yet published, probably knows the truth. Some day we may all know it.

An interesting chapter of speculation might be written meanwhile; for Marguerite lives as clearly in her lover's description as do most heroines in literature, but this bypath is not for us. It is the poetry she evoked that is our concern. The poems would make a little volume by themselves. They include not only the seven poems which are collected under the title, *Switzerland*, but also the five poems called *Faded Leaves* in the 1855 edition, *The Voice* published 1849, the poem called *A Dream* which was finally placed among the "early poems", the poem called *A Memory Picture* once included in the *Switzerland* group, but now included in the "early poems", *The New Sirens* of which Arnold wrote a rather mystifying paraphrase to his friend Clough, as though it had to do with literary criticism only, and the masterpiece already mentioned, *The Forsaken Merman*. Some have thought that there are many other allusions to Marguerite. Professor Garrod and Sir Edmund Chambers think there is a recollection of her in *Tristram and Iseult*—which is to be sure very possible, for it is a poem of unhappy love. I have no doubt that present-day psychologists would press the matter to great lengths, and might even connect Marguerite with Arnold's whimsies about the Deceased Wife's Sister Bill. But let us confine ourselves to poems which we are sure Marguerite shapes and inspires, seventeen poems. They are very uneven. Clough called *The New Sirens* a "mumble", and Arnold cordially agreed. He rejected the poem entitled *The Voice* from his 1869 edition, calling it falsetto, but it is worth reading as part of Arnold, and as one of his experiments in poetry. *A Memory Picture* is interesting only for biographical purposes, not as poetry. The seven poems which Arnold wisely saw to have a coherence, and which were finally grouped together in *Switzerland*, are all poetry. The second one, called *Parting*, is tempestuous and passionate, and unlike the ordinary accepted view of Arnold. One of the group, like *The Forsaken Merman*, is a masterpiece. I quote it as the shortest way to confute a fairly common criticism of Arnold's love poetry and of his lyric gift:

> Yes! in the sea of life enisled,
> With echoing straits between us thrown,
> Dotting the shoreless watery wild,
> We mortal millions live alone.
> The islands feel the enclasping flow,
> And then their endless bounds they know.
>
> But when the moon their hollows lights,
> And they are swept by balms of spring,

> And in their glens, on starry nights,
> The nightingales divinely sing;
> And lovely notes, from shore to shore,
> Across the sounds and channels pour—
>
> Oh! then a longing like despair
> Is to their farthest caverns sent;
> For surely once, they feel, we were
> Parts of a single continent!
> Now round us spreads the watery plain—
> Oh might our marges meet again!
>
> Who order'd, that their longing's fire
> Should be, as soon as kindled, cool'd?
> Who renders vain their deep desire?
> A God, a God their severance ruled!
> And bade betwixt their shores to be
> The unplumb'd, salt, estranging sea.

The five poems called *Faded Leaves* also have a coherence, and are poetry, but one of them stands out, *On the Rhine*; though one could not give it the high praise which is due to the poem just quoted, and to *The Forsaken Merman*.

But we have not yet dealt with all the great poetry of the 1849 edition. It contains the much admired poem, very characteristic of Arnold, called *Resignation*. Its scene is the lake country where Arnold spent his schoolboy holidays, and where Wordsworth was still living on. Its reminiscence of Wordsworth is, therefore, hardly accidental. And yet, to the reader of all three poets, *Resignation* is much more deeply reminiscent of

Lucretius than of Wordsworth; and I am pleased that I detected this long before I knew that Arnold was a lifelong student of Lucretius, and for twenty years worked on a tragedy on that subject. (It is worth while remembering that Lucretius himself had a great affection for Empedocles, the Sicilian poet and physician.) Since no one seems to have observed the Lucretian ring in *Resignation*, let us pause for a moment to give one or two clues. Here is a characteristic couplet in Lucretius:

> Alid ex alio reficit Natura nec ullam
> Rem gigni patitur nisi morte adjuta aliena.

Again, one might cite passages in Lucretius on the vanity of prayer, on the vanity of passion, the pain of birth, the supreme desirability of security of mind,[2] and the theory which Lucretius took from Empedocles, that the universe moves and lasts by repulsion and attraction—whence the great passage on the marriage of Mars and Venus:

> The world in which we live and move
> Outlasts aversion, outlasts love.

And yet, when all is said, neither Wordsworth nor Lucretius is obtrusively apparent in *Resignation*. Further, in this poem, even more than in *Mycerinus* or *The Forsaken Merman*, the Matthew Arnold that we are later to know shines forth. It is not merely the fondness for upland waters

---

[2] The ἀταραξία of Epicurus—Lucretius' master.

and scenery, for the careless freedom of gypsy life; here is plainly struck the elegiac strain, and here is plainly the idyllic background:

> He sees the gentle stir of birth
> When morning purifies the earth;
> He leans upon a gate and sees
> The pastures, and the quiet trees.
> Low, woody hill, with gracious bound,
> Folds the still valley almost round;
> The cuckoo, loud on some high lawn,
> Is answer'd from the depth of dawn;
> In the hedge straggling to the stream,
> Pale, dew-drench'd, half-shut roses gleam;
> But, where the farther side slopes down,
> He sees the drowsy new-waked clown
> In his white quaint-embroider'd frock
> Make, whistling, tow'rd his mist-wreathed flock—
> Slowly, behind his heavy tread,
> The wet, flower'd grass heaves up its head.

The only direct allusion to the Greeks, in the poem, is to breathing Homer's "immortal air", but there is more, indirectly, of Theocritus—a foreshadowing, if you will, of *The Scholar Gipsy*, *Thyrsis*, and the perhaps still later *Bacchanalia*. But it is a Theocritus transformed, a more English breath in it, I believe, than in either Milton or Shelley. More notable than these things is the emergence of Matthew Arnold as we are later to know him, sure that the poet must go on, in his "rapt security", whatever faith may have fallen from him, and yet with a wistful glance backward at the beauty and serenity of that faith:

> Tears
> Are in his eyes, and in his ears
> The murmur of a thousand years.

Again, the poem moves on from the mere renunciation that some have seen in *The New Sirens*, and that is plain in the early Marguerite poems. I am inclined to believe, though I cannot be sure in our present state of knowledge, that when *Resignation* was written (it was published February 26, 1849) the Marguerite episode was definitely over, even though he was to have a fearful agitation in Switzerland in the following September.[3] At any rate it is plain that now Arnold sees "the high white star of Truth" clear before him.

We now proceed to the poems published in 1852. *Empedocles on Etna*, which gave the title to the collection, leads straight on from *Resignation*, the most mature poem in the 1849 edition. The uplands of the lake country have become the Sicilian Mountains, we have now arrived in the

---

[3] Sir Edmund Chambers, arguing from *The Voice*, also published early in 1849, says that the episode was over, and that hereupon "Arnold dedicates himself to his high calling, and also to the routine of the Education Office". As for the latter, it was more than two years afterwards that Arnold took up his duties in the Education Office. Into such lapses does the difficulty of the chronology of Arnold's poems lead one!

very land of Theocritus; though, in view of the subject, we are not so much aware of Theocritus as of Lucretius, through whom we best know Empedocles. There is quoted also a fragment of Parmenides, and we catch more than an accent of Plato and the Sophists of the fifth century B.C. *Empedocles* is not one of Arnold's most successful poems. Thrown into a dramatic form, it is not dramatic enough; to that extent we must share Arnold's own criticism of it. But it contains beautiful lyrics, some fine blank verse; and it is a stage in Arnold's development; it expresses as he has not yet done the longing of the philosopher to master his own soul and yet his discontent to leave the mass of contentious and blindly struggling men to their own fate. He had already touched on this in *Obermann*, which, though it appeared in the *Empedocles* collection, was written in 1849. From solitude in the cool beauty of the mountain glens Empedocles returns to the hot and dusty cities of the plain, from a sense of duty; but once again disgust drives him out to his own airy meditations. Did Arnold think of Plato oscillating between the grove of the Academy in Athens and the tyrant's court in Syracuse? He makes little attempt, naturally, in this poem to anglicize the Greek Muses. It is sometimes said that Gray lurks in his mind when he describes the eagle of Zeus, but of course Arnold knew Pindar as well as he knew Gray. In the songs of Callicles there echo the choruses of the Attic tragedians. But it is Arnold's own philosophy that emerges in the concluding stanzas of Empedocles' chant, though it has a very Lucretian ring:

> Is it so small a thing
> To have enjoy'd the sun,
> To have lived light in the spring,
> To have loved, to have thought, to have done;
> To have advanced true friends, and beat down
>   baffling foes—
>
> That we must feign a bliss
> Of doubtful future date,
> And, while we dream on this,
> Lose all our present state,
> And relegate to worlds yet distant our repose?
>
> Not much, I know, you prize
> What pleasures may be had,
> Who look on life with eyes
> Estranged, like mine, and sad;
> And yet the village-churl feels the truth more
>   than you,
>
> Who's loath to leave this life
> Which to him little yields—
> His hard-task'd sunburnt wife,
> His often-labour'd fields,
> The boors with whom he talk'd, the country-
>   spots he knew.
>
> But thou, because thou hear'st
> Men scoff at Heaven and Fate,

> Because the Gods thou fear'st
> Fail to make blest thy state,
> Tremblest, and wilt not dare to trust the joys
>   there are!
>
> I say: Fear Not! Life still
> Leaves human effort scope.
> But, since life teems with ill,
> Nurse no extravagant hope;
> Because thou must not dream, thou need'st not
>   then despair!

After this, in the apostrophe to the stars we have a thought often expressed in other poems—*A Summer Night, Self-Dependence, Morality*; and towards the end, in a more prosaic passage, perhaps it should be called, a prognostication of the doctrine of "sweetness and light":

>   Slave of sense
> I have in no wise been;—but slave of thought?
> And who can say: I have been always free,
> Lived ever in the light of my own soul?—
> I cannot; I have lived in wrath and gloom,
> Fierce, disputatious, ever at war with man,
> Far from my own soul, far from warmth and light
> But I have not grown easy in these bonds—
> But I have not denied what bonds these were.
> Yea, I take myself to witness,
> That I have loved no darkness,
> Sophisticated no truth,
> Nursed no delusion,
> Allow'd no fear!

The poem concludes with the much quoted hymn of Callicles. This is very beautiful, but perhaps Arnold regarded it as a purple patch, in his deep dissatisfaction with the poem which Browning so much admired.

Tristram and Iseult, though its theme is congenial to Arnold (some imagine that it confirms a hint in another poem that Marguerite was a married woman), is not one of Arnold's successes. He does not move at ease in mediaeval legend. This was not merely his own temper, but was the temper of his age. Neither Morris nor Tennyson revived the mediaeval time in any convincing way. The nineteenth century, especially after the first few decades, was much closer to the fifth century B.C. than it was to the seventeenth century A.D., to say nothing of the Middle Ages. Keats alone, perhaps, of the Moderns, could open this door, but Keats was a "throw-back", an Elizabethan almost in temper, as Arnold perhaps imperfectly saw. It was a bootless task to berate Keats for being what he was, instead of gratefully accepting him, but it was worth while to warn others against imitating an anachronism. With *Tristram and Iseult*, Arnold turned his own back on it, though later he gave it one more wistful glance.[4] There is seemingly a brief return to it in *Saint Brandan*, which was first published in

---
[4]*Stanzas from the Grande Chartreuse*, pub. 1855.

Fraser's Magazine in 1860. But I do not know when this was written. It is a silly poem.

The Buried Life, not so well known as many of his other poems, is one of Arnold's most perfect. It concludes with a metaphor of which he was very fond; he had already used it in *A Dream*, and he is to use it again:

> And then he thinks he knows
> The hills where his life rose,
> And the sea where it goes.

But this metaphor glances away somewhat from the main thought of the poem. *That* thought, or something like it, is to be found in a few lines in the *Cornhill* article, "St. Paul and Protestantism", November, 1869. The lines were his own, but he nowhere republished them, nor acknowledged them:

> Below the surface stream, shallow and light,
> Of what we say we feel, below the stream
> As light, of what we think we feel, there flows
> With noiseless current strong, obscure and deep,
> The central stream of what we feel indeed.

The *Stanzas in Memory of the Author of "Obermann"* are chiefly interesting, I think, as a revelation of Arnold's mind in the important year 1849. Not published till 1852, the author dated them November, 1849. He had to do so because the poem refers to Wordsworth as still living, and

Wordsworth died in 1850. But the poem in part at least must have been composed before November, 1849, for Arnold quotes from it in a letter in September of that year. If we remember that, and the last visit to Marguerite that same month, we can more easily understand the long drawn-out and passionate farewell to the shade of the dead author whom he calls his guide. It runs over two pages, beginning:

> Away!
> Away the dreams that but deceive,
> And thou, sad guide, adieu!
> I go, fate drives me; but I leave
> Half of my life with you.

and concludes,

> Farewell, under the sky we part
> In the stern Alpine dell.
> O unstrung will! O broken heart!
> A last, a last farewell!

Like *Resignation* this poem also looks forward to Empedocles' dilemma:

> Ah! two desires toss about
> The poet's feverish blood.
> One drives him to the world without,
> And one to solitude.

The poem, *Obermann*, connects Wordsworth and Goethe with the obscure French writer, de Senancour (1770-1846), whereas *Memorial Verses* connect them with Byron. The latter combination, so often criticized, is perhaps not stranger than the other.

In the 1852 collection is a group of poems which look not merely back to Wordsworth in part, and Arnold's youth, but forward to his prose works on religion: *The Youth of Nature, The Youth of Man, Progress, Self-Dependence, Morality*. Though consolation for human doubt and pain is their theme, one feels rather the doubt and pain. The concluding poem of the book, however, *The Future*, succeeds where they fail; it succeeds also in being poetry.

We have now dealt with the main poems of the 1849 and 1852 collections. Both were apparently still-born, so far as the reviews were concerned; and Arnold, who had not signed them, quietly withdrew them, the second almost instantly through dissatisfaction with *Empedocles*. Some have expressed surprise that neither volume received popular acclaim. But is it surprising? The public had not yet accepted Keats; Wordsworth had not yet found his sure fame—which Arnold's criticism was largely to give him. It has been said that Tennyson attained reputation with his 1842 collection, but Tennyson had had to wait. Besides Tennyson was more in line with public taste, by reason of his prettiness and ornament,—a style which in painting as well as in poetry the Victorian Age was unfortunately to approve. Arnold, restrained, even austere, quite failed to hit such a taste. Again, the thought of Tennyson is simple and shallow, with no suspicion of a challenge to orthodoxy. Though lucid, Arnold's thought is not shallow, and from the first he must have given uneasiness to the ordinary and conventional mind. The surprising thing in any age would have been the instant acclaim of Arnold's work. To be sure Goldwin Smith gave instant praise to *Mycerinus*; Browning to *Empedocles*; Swinburne (characteristically) to the much more doubtful beauties of *The New Sirens*. And we have heard Froude on *The Forsaken Merman*. This surely was a good beginning; and there must have been other readers who were aware from this first work that a star of great magnitude had risen.

Meantime Arnold was steadily engaged in poetic work, revising, reading, meditating. Hardly had he withdrawn *Empedocles* when he began to write *Sohrab and Rustum*. This time, the only time, I think, we can follow the progress of his composition in his letters, brief as the allusions are. On May 1, 1853, he writes to Clough: "I have just got through a thing which pleases me better than anything I have yet done." On July 27, he was already quoting from the eighteenth stanza of *The Scholar Gipsy*. On August 3: "I have written out my Sohrab and Rustum, and like it less." On October 10: "The Preface is done. . . . How difficult it is to write prose: and why? because of the *articulations of the discourse*: one leaps these over in Poetry—places one thought cheek by jowl with another without introducing them and leaves them—but in prose this will not do. It is of course not right in poetry either—but we all do it." The *Poems* of 1853, with the famous prose Preface, appeared in November. For the first time he signed his work. *Empedocles* did not reappear, and the Preface explained why.

Let us defer the Preface to a later lecture and look at *Sohrab and Rustum*. In many ways it stands out, as anyone can see, from anything he has yet done.

When critics ask carpingly: "What does Arnold mean by the grand style?" we can always send them back to examples of it which he culled from other poetry, but we can also advise them to read his own work, *Sohrab and Rustum*. For here it is: not merely an imitation of the grandeur of Homer, but a lofty poem in its own right, where Arnold fuses the swift impulses and hopes of man, his noble pity and enduring tragic sense. He does this not only with a scholar's lore, recalling as nothing else does that crowning glory of the *Iliad*, Priam begging Achilles for the body of Hector, but also with Arnold's own subtlest and grandest use of his peculiar metaphor—the likening of an individual life and human experience at large to a great river, eager and tumultuous in youth, majestic in middle course, at the end resignedly and even gladly merging itself in infinite tides. Here, too, is grand action, which Arnold desiderated both in *Empedocles* and to a less extent, as we shall see, in *The Scholar Gipsy*. The two great characters are of heroic mould and in the background sits Fate, an ἔφεδρος, waiting to conquer conqueror and conquered alike. The scenery is managed not as Homer and Milton manage it, but with the vague grandeur of Aeschylus: so remote from most of us is this vast expanse of the highlands and steppes of central Asia that we feel, as we do in reading the *Prometheus*, that we are on the rim of the world; and the effect is heightened by allusions to lonely hunters, to eagles viewing inaccessible precipices, and to caravans struggling over passes too difficult even for birds. Yet in these stern wastes is seen the passion of man, for lucre mainly, but among the nobler for glory and enduring fame. Homeric it is, in diction and simile, in simplicity and directness. But its delicate use of irony reminds one rather of the Attic tragedies. One admires, too, the Persian and Oriental lore, already foreshadowed in the earlier poems, the *Strayed Reveller, Resignation, Consolation.*

It is then, if you will, a scholar's poem, and the scholarly reader has, I suppose, sometimes asked himself what the comparatively illiterate reader can make of Arnold and of Milton. And most readers to-day, nay, nearly all that vast throng of men and women who essay "Eng. Lit.", are not scholars. They sit poring, ostensibly over treasures, but really over barren foot-notes, which also in the main have been compiled not by scholars; thrice removed from the mountain springs and mountain air by their unwillingness, and the unwillingness of the past generation who are their teachers, for arduous but heaven-rewarded toil. And they ask, sitting on cushions as they roll along the vulgar highway, and chatting with critics as soft as themselves: "What is the grand style?"

"But surely", it may be asked, "surely the conclusion of the poem can be enjoyed by those who are innocent of scholarship? For that is Arnold himself, his highly original self, with no apparent imitation of Greeks or anyone else?" But can the conclusion be read by itself? Great poetry cannot be gobbeted and sampled in this fashion. Great poetry, as readers of Arnold at least should know, is not a cento of pretty bits: its effect is a total effect. Besides Arnold is not many things by turns, poet, scholar, critic, but one and the same Arnold throughout. Those who complain so heatedly about his academic robes, about the professor of poetry or the political reformer crushing out the poet, reveal only their own littleness of soul. Some of them, riding their own theories to death, make the most egregious mis-statements through failure even to study the chronology of Arnold's work.

The Scholar Gipsy is another bugbear to some critics. But let us leave them and look at the poem. It was written and published in 1853, though probably the theme was turned over in Arnold's deliberate fashion long before. It is redolent of Oxford, an earlier Oxford, the Oxford Arnold knew and which some of us were fortunate enough to know before modern traffic began its improvement and destruction. It has the idyllic background of several of Arnold's poems, his model up to nearly the end of the poem being Theocritus and the other pastoral writers of the Alexandrian Age. And, once again, despite the English scene which so many Englishmen have loved, despite the Greek reminiscences, the poem is Arnold himself. It is indeed largely so characteristic of a side of Arnold, which he tried hard to escape—the dominant mood in Clough from which, to Arnold's great sorrow, Clough never recovered—that he was afterwards, for a time at least, ashamed of the poem; especially was he so when Clough praised it. I think it helps us to appreciate the poem when we know this. That is not to say that the poem from first line to last does not explain itself. I have always thought it a little stupid to complain that the mood and atmosphere of the concluding stanzas are unlike the mood and atmosphere earlier in the poem. They are meant to be unlike—that is the whole point! Any classical student knows, of course, that with the resolute "Tyrian trader" Arnold forsakes the inspiration of the decadent Alexandrian poets and recalls the spacious Mediterranean world of Herodotus. And these students remember too, that the great days of expansion for the Greeks were cramping days for the Phoenicians. Historically, as well as in Arnold's fancy, some of them sped resolutely away to expand a new empire in the remote West. This is the whole point of the simile which concludes the poem. It is not merely that Arnold braces himself after indulging in a melancholy mood, and lamenting the past; the moral is that even in this age there are worlds of great things to do.

Let us pick up the thread I dropped a moment ago, and explain the allusion to Clough. It is clear, I think, that Clough missed the meaning of the poem, and Arnold was in considerable agitation lest the poem was in general a failure. In enlightening Clough, in a letter which seems to me a model of delicacy, and which ought to be a lightning flash through the murky obscurity of critics, Arnold reveals himself and the core of his poetry. Unfortunately, it was not until 1932 that Professor Lowry published this correspondence.

On November 30, 1853, Arnold writes to Clough:

> I am glad you like the Gipsy Scholar—but what does it *do* for you? Homer *animates*—Shakespeare *animates*—in its poor way I think Sohrab and Rustum *animates*—the Gipsy Scholar at best awakens a pleasing melancholy. But this is not what we want.
>
> > The complaining millions of men
> > Darken in labour and pain—

(here, by the way, he quotes from his own poem, *The Youth of Nature*)

> what they want is something to *animate* and ennoble them—not merely to add zest to their melancholy or grace to their dreams.—I believe a feeling of this kind is the basis of my nature—and of my poetics.
>
> You certainly do not seem to me sufficiently to desire and earnestly strive towards—assured knowledge—activity—happiness. You are too content to *fluctuate*—to be ever learning, never coming to the knowledge of the truth. This is why, with you, I feel it necessary to stiffen myself—and hold fast my rudder.
>
> My poems, however, viewed *absolutely*, are certainly little or nothing.

Now, this is very modest indeed, and not too

pointed. We have to remember that Arnold is writing to a very intimate and valued friend, his senior by nearly four years, who had published poetry before himself, and to a favourite pupil of his father, who only a few short years ago, as a family friend, had held an almost paternal relationship to himself. Arnold cannot tell Clough, even if he would, that he has missed the point of the poem. The language is generalized, and the innuendo wrapped in many words. But it is no coincidence that after condemning the scholar's quest and the repining for a lost world, in a new world of darkening and complaining millions, he describes himself as laying hold of that very implement, the rudder, which the "Tyrian trader" snatches up to sail to a new West. True, he softens the remark for Clough by saying *"with you* I stiffen myself and hold fast my rudder".

Now, some pert little critics of our day say that Arnold is a Victorian prude, that he could not be content with poetry, but must make poetry of some use. But did not Wordsworth praise Milton for his "soul-animating strains"? And was not Milton conscious of his soul-animating strains? It was said recently in an extravagant eulogy of Swinburne[5] that Plato, in demanding that poetry be moral, and Matthew Arnold, following Plato,

---
[5]Randolph Hughes, "A. C. Swinburne, a Centenary Survey" (*Nineteenth Century*, June, 1937).

had wrenched the purpose of poetry awry. But what of Shelley's account of poetry, and Philip Sidney's before him? What said Aristophanes (surely not a prude!) even before Plato's time? What if these now current notions were applied to Homer, or Sophocles, or Shakespeare? Is Shakespeare a mere tinkle of music, an artist for art's sake, or did he blow a soul-animating strain? Such questions answer themselves. The reason that so much of Arnold will endure is that he demanded of himself what he admired in the great poets of the past: nobility of thought and perfection of style.

The 1853 volume, we may note in passing, gave Arnold an assured position with the more serious readers of the day. He had now really won through. Smaller things, but of a perfect kind, *Strew on her Roses, Roses*, had an even wider appeal, and his reputation steadily grew.

The 1855 volume contained as novelties *Balder Dead* and one of the Marguerite poems, written long before, *Separation*. The best that can be said for *Balder Dead* is that there are fine bits in it, and that, according to Arnold's own canons, is to damn it. Arnold is not the only one who has made a valiant attempt to revive our supposed Norse ancestors and make us admire them.[6] In comparison with Norse mythology Milton's theme

---

[6] What is one to say of Wagner's work, even of *Lohengrin*?

is intensely familiar to us, nor is Homer's mythology alien to a European. But the Norse mythology is as remote from us, as exotic, as Chinese poetry. Perhaps more so, being humourless. Arnold thought perhaps that the gods of the Vikings might win our sympathy if he made them talk Homerically. But you can teach an Eskimo French and yet fail to interest a Frenchman in what an Eskimo has to say. It is in such a place as this that Arnold's lack of historic sense appears. Two years later, in his first Oxford lecture, he was to set forth the close relationship of Periclean Athens with contemporary England, and to argue that Thucydides stood closer to us than the historical work of Walter Raleigh. This sort of thing Arnold's father might have said. But Matthew Arnold failed to see the implication of this when writing *Balder Dead*. For *Balder Dead* he made this apology to Palgrave: "We have enough Scandinavian in our nature and history to make a short conspectus of the Scandinavian mythology admissible." A modest statement; but, I think, not true.

Merope, a tragedy in the Attic manner, is another failure. It was written as a sort of inauguration of his professorship of Poetry at Oxford, 1857, and published the following year. It does not succeed in being an English poem. Some classical scholars admired it, though Browning did not, and Arnold himself continued to admire it. A Greek scholar reading it for the first time may admire it as a skilfully manufactured play. Given the setting he knows what to expect, and Arnold does not fail him, as he constructs scene on scene. But it is not a *Samson Agonistes*: it lacks inspiration.

III

ARNOLD'S POETRY (continued)

WE come now to the *New Poems*, published in 1867. One of the earliest, and perhaps the earliest, of these is *Stanzas from the Grande Chartreuse*. It had already appeared in *Fraser's Magazine* in 1855. The poetry is characteristic in several ways, as we realize when we plunge into it: we are on a rainy Alpine mountainside, by which one climbs with a guide to the monastery. This is scenery in which Arnold is always at home. And not only is it a beautiful poem, it is as intimate a revelation of his own soul as Arnold has anywhere given us. Here there is resolution as well as dirge. The "rigorous teachers" who "seized his youth" and pointed to him the "high white Star of Truth" he has not deserted, nor ever will. He has a resolute hope also that another firm rock for his faith will one day be found. But lament is the dominant note in his present mood. Few are left in the world with the faith of the Carthusians, and he is not one of those few. He sorrows only between two worlds, "one dead, one powerless to be born". The men of action, however, heedless and thoughtless, are not for him. His tears he will rather mingle with the faith and prayers of those who still adhere to a creed outworn—outworn for himself and most of his fellow-men.

> Sons of the world, oh, speed those years;
> But, while we wait, allow our tears!
>
> Allow them! We admire with awe
> The exulting thunder of your race;
> You give the universe your law,
> You triumph over time and space!
> Your pride of life, your tireless powers,
> We laud them, but they are not ours.
>
> We are like children rear'd in shade
> Beneath some old-world abbey wall,
> Forgotten in a forest-glade,
> And secret from the eyes of all.

And then he follows this simile with bold metaphor, transplanting us into the Middle Ages with a skill hardly seen in *Tristram and Iseult*, and perhaps, to a fastidious critic, somewhat marring the unity of the poem by leaving us there, instead of bringing us back to the world where we belong:

> We are like children rear'd in shade
> Beneath some old-world abbey wall,
> Forgotten in a forest-glade,
> And secret from the eyes of all.

Now, mark the bold transition:

> Deep, deep the greenwood round them waves,
> Their abbey, and its close of graves!
>
> But, where the road runs near the stream,
> Oft through the trees they catch a glance

Of passing troops in the sun's beam—
Pennon, and plume, and flashing lance!
Forth to the world those soldiers fare,
To life, to cities, and to war!

And through the wood, another way,
Faint bugle-notes from far are borne,
Where hunters gather, staghounds bay,
Round some fair forest-lodge at morn.
Gay dames are there, in sylvan green;
Laughter and cries—those notes between!

The banners flashing through the trees
Make their blood dance and chain their eyes,
That bugle-music on the breeze
Arrests them with a charm'd surprise.
Banner by turns and bugle woo:
Ye shy recluses, follow too!

O children, what do ye reply?—
"Action and pleasure, will ye roam
Through these secluded dells to cry
And call us?—but too late ye come!
Too late for us your call ye blow,
Whose bent was taken long ago.

"Long since we pace this shadow'd nave;
We watch those yellow tapers shine,
Emblems of hope over the grave,
In the high altar's depth divine;
The organ carries to our ear
Its accents of another sphere.

"Fenced early in this cloistral round
Of reverie, of shade, of prayer,
How should we grow in other ground?

How can we flower in foreign air?
—Pass, banners, pass, and bugles, cease;
And leave our desert to its peace!"

Well, it is a very beautiful close, and perhaps some admirers of Arnold will not thank us for finding any fault with it. But it is Arnold himself, Arnold and the Greeks, who have taught us to desiderate unity here. And we should have studied him ill, either in example or precept, did we not remark on this.

As against this criticism, I am well aware, it might be claimed that the poet's aim is not only deliberate, but well thought out: that here Arnold is like the poet in *Resignation*,

> Tears
> Are in his eyes, and in his ears
> The murmur of a thousand years;

that, in mingling his tears with the prayers of the Carthusians, he is rapt away to their world, which is really mediaeval. To be sure he is thus rapt away, and I am ready to admit that most probably Arnold concludes the poem as he does of set purpose. But I think the unity and consistency I crave, which Arnold elsewhere exhibits, could have been secured by the addition of a single stanza,—a stanza, for example, depicting the poet descending the bleak, rainy mountain-side, to face once more the life of the plain.

Dover Beach is on the same theme, and was,

perhaps, written about the same time. I cannot be sure of this, but I observe that Arnold holidayed at Dover in 1854, and again in 1856. It is perhaps one of the most cited of his poems in our time; in fact I have heard Arnold described as "the author of *Dover Beach* and similar pieces". It is, to be sure, characteristic; but as we have seen he has many other moods. Like so much of Arnold's best work in both verse and prose it includes lines and phrases which give promise of passing into the language: "the eternal note of sadness", "the Sea of Faith was once, too, at the full", "the naked shingles of the world", "where ignorant armies clash by night". From his melancholy Arnold sometimes retreats on Stoicism for reinforcement; sometimes on a resolve to accomplish an amelioration of human life or human thought. Here, as someone has said, he withdraws himself into conjugal affection and happiness, which in his case was notoriously complete. A very beautiful poem.

Rugby Chapel bears the date, November, 1857. This is another illustration of the difficulty in being certain of the exact time when any of Arnold's work was composed. It is, of course, an author's privilege to ask us to believe that a poem was composed on an anniversary date, or any other date, whether it was or not. In this case when the poem was published, in 1867, and his mother approved of it, Arnold told her that he had conceived it on reading Fitzjames Stephen's review of *Tom Brown's Schooldays* in the *Edinburgh Review* (Stephen wrote of Dr. Arnold as a humourless, bustling fanatic, who made little prigs of all his charges). Now, that article appeared in 1858, so the poem must have been composed after that time.

I confess that *Rugby Chapel* is not one of the poems that I most admire. I think it is a noble tribute, doing infinite credit to father and son alike, but hesitate to say that it is "a worthy example" of Arnold's elegiac gift. Some who deride his unrhymed short-line poems think that he triumphs here. I cannot go that length. But perhaps the severest critic of Dr. Arnold would admit that his son, who had five years under him at Rugby, and twenty years of him at home, is neither prig nor weakling, but a manly, leal, and devoted soldier in the cause of Truth as he saw it. Matthew Arnold's private saying about his father, "dear Dr. Arnold was not infallible", has been sometimes thought to be a trifle inconsistent. But Matthew's letters to his mother, who long outlived her husband, should be read. There Arnold always took it for granted that his father had been in the van of reform in religious thought as in everything else, and that had he lived longer he would have gone farther in reform. Certainly Dr.

Arnold's widow kept abreast of the times, and indeed, from her son's letters, would seem to have grown continuously younger.

Nor is *Rugby Chapel* to be considered merely as the outburst of a man who has seen his clan attacked. Writing to his mother, seven years after Fitzjames Stephen's article appeared, he said of his father: "His greatness consisted in bringing such a torrent of freshness into English religion, by placing history and politics in connection with it." Elsewhere he speaks of his own life's work as being simply a continuation of his father's. Certainly they were both great moral and religious teachers; certainly they were both great educational reformers, and both laid hold on the excellent and abiding examples of thought in the past: Thomas Arnold on Thucydides, one of the greatest thinkers of all time; his son on Homer, Herodotus, and Sophocles, who are among the most gracious human spirits of all time. Both were in earnest, terrifically in earnest; both would have thought the saying, "Surtout point de zêle", a blasphemy against Heaven, and a craven's excuse. But neither was a Puritan nor a fanatic, and collectively they show a good humour and good sense which hardly any other pair of men in their century can muster, whether we consider Carlyle and Ruskin, Darwin and Huxley, the two Mills, Chamberlain and Morley.

Thyrsis was written in Arnold's forty-fourth year, perhaps eighteen years after he first gave promise of great poetry, indeed twenty-two years or more after the sonnet on Shakespeare; fifteen years after he became school inspector, thirteen years after his first published prose, nine years after his professorship. These facts are worth recording, with some emphasis, because one so often reads that his Muse visited him for only a brief period—ten years at most, some say—; and that the fountain of inspiration was choked in him by official duties, by criticism, by academic lecturing. True, thirteen years earlier he complained to Clough, and to his sister, how difficult he found it to compose *Sohrab and Rustum* at white heat, so many were his interruptions. And interruptions in the long interval had increased. But nothing of Arnold's work is more perfect than *Thyrsis*; to my thinking little in English poetry is more perfect. I once heard a poet of our day— to whose work the saying has some application— say that if a man enriched his native tongue by a single perfect poem, short or long, that was all the world should demand of him. If Arnold had written nothing but *Thyrsis*, how great would be our debt to him! Much of Arnold is here: his rich scholarship, his love of natural beauty, his striving for perfection in life, his ardent desire for companionship in the great quest, his scorn of worldliness, pettiness, and vulgar greed, and his abiding melancholy. Unlike Milton, he refrains from laying aside his Dorian reed for a trumpet. He knows what the pastoral ditty can bear, and he says in one of his letters that *Thyrsis* is "a very quiet poem". How completely English he has made his Greek lore here! There are cadences which only the scholar catches; that will always be so, no doubt, while English poetry continues to be written; and there is a ripe wisdom in *Thyrsis* which only a man of rich and varied experience can appreciate. And yet it can cast a spell over anyone, young or old, who is in the least capable of being magnetized by the Muses. For how many poems dare a sober and well-read critic make such claims! Twice, perhaps, in his life, Andrew Lang, who had a hard side, and who generally wrote in a borrowed style, melted and gave himself to Apollo; once when he recalled his gray college:

> St. Andrews, by the Northern Sea
> A haunted town it is to me!

And once, when completely inspired, he felt the spell of *Thyrsis*:

> The wail of Moschus on the mountains crying
>   The Muses heard, and loved it long ago;
> They heard the hollows of the hills replying,
>   They heard the weeping water's overflow;
> They winged the sacred strain—the song undying,
>   The song that all about the world must go—

> When poets for a poet dead are sighing,
>   The minstrels for a minstrel friend laid low.
>
> And dirge to dirge that answers, and the weeping
>   For Adonais by the summer sea;
> The plaints for Lycidas and Thyrsis (sleeping
>   Far from "the forest ground called Thessaly");
> These hold thy memory, Bion, in their keeping,
>   And are but echoes of the moan for thee.

It surprises me to find that *Bacchanalia* is a favourite with Arnold's critics, and to hear it spoken of as one of his most beautiful poems. The opening is indeed beautiful; this is in the idyllic manner, which Arnold could handle perfectly always, either in his earlier or later period. (We cannot be sure of the date of *Bacchanalia*, but perhaps it is as late as anything in the 1867 collection.) But the allegory which follows seems to me a little forced and artificial, and the satire towards the end jars with the quiet and beautiful beginning. One does not complain, of course, of two moods appearing in a poem, or many moods, but the poem must prepare one for the change, and be consistent and an artistic unity. I have defended the change of mood in *The Scholar Gipsy*, but in this poem the reader is, I think, left groping, and guessing by the change.

Obermann Once More is also a late poem in this collection. One stanza in it almost everyone knows:

> The East bow'd low before the blast
> In patient, deep disdain;
> She let the legions thunder past,
> And plunged in thought again.

But seemingly few who quote the stanza know its origin, and about the poem as a whole there would seem to be almost a conspiracy of silence. Has the unorthodoxy of the long address of Obermann, heard by Arnold in a vision, anything to do with this? Swinburne praised it, and, as Arnold knew, Swinburne was a dangerous ally. He wrote to his mother about it, November, 1867, and complained too that Church publications and orthodox writers in other papers "fix on the speeches of Empedocles and Obermann and calmly say, dropping all mention of the real speakers, 'Mr. Arnold here professes his pantheism', or 'Mr. Arnold here disowns Christianity' ".

The poem is beautifully composed, to use that word in Arnold's own technical sense. The poet finds himself, after an absence of twenty years, in a part of Switzerland which has for him many associations. Pensively he notes the changes in the immediate foreground, and then one by one he remarks on the things unchanged, and exclaims:

> The cone of Jaman, pale and grey,
> See, in the blue profound!
>
> Ah, Jaman! delicately tall
> Above his sun-warm'd firs—

> What thoughts to me his rocks recall,
> What memories he stirs!

The memories are of Obermann, one of the guides of his youth, and of Marguerite, let us say in parenthesis. While he muses on this and his life since, night falls, and as he lies on the grass beside a mountain chalet Obermann appears to him in a dream; exclaims at his return, and proceeds to compare the present with the Roman world in the days just before Christ. (The description of the *ennui* of this Roman life is, by the way, borrowed from Lucretius—whose life fell in this period.) We are then transported to the brooding East, the cradle of religions, and the "victorious West" is described as listening to the Orient, with its "new-born joy". Obermann laments:

> Oh, had I lived in that great day,
> How had its glory new
> Fill'd earth and heaven, and caught away
> My ravish'd spirit too!

"But", after many centuries,

> But slow that tide of common thought,
> Which bathed our life, retired;
> Slow, slow the old world wore to nought,
> And pulse by pulse expired.

Men prayed for a freshening storm; there came the French Revolution. From the sham world which followed,—men feebly piecing together the worn-out rites and dead creeds,—Obermann had fled to the Alpine snows, a recluse. Here Arnold in his youth had discovered his writing. Now a new world is at hand, and he bids Arnold proclaim it.

> Though more than half thy years be past,
> And spent thy youthful prime;
> Though, round thy firmer manhood cast,
> Hang weeds of our sad time
>
> Whereof thy youth felt all the spell,
> And traversed all the shade—
> Though late, though dimm'd, though weak, yet tell
> Hope to a world new-made!

And he gives hints of what the gospel must be. Arnold wakes, hears no voice but the torrent below, sees again the peak of Jaman among the stars, and looks about from peak to peak. Finally:

> And glorious there, without a sound,
> Across the glimmering lake,
> High in the Valais-depth profound,
> I saw the morning break.

I have said so much about this poem for several reasons. It is not well enough known by those who write about Arnold. In plan and execution it is very beautiful. Those, too, who think of Arnold as the author of *Dover Beach*, would see another side to him here. And aside from its own intrinsic beauties the poem should be read, for in it Arnold, in sketch at least, reviews his whole poetic career up to the age of forty-five.

Nearly fifteen years after the 1867 collection, which many think the last poems of Arnold, he published a very striking poem called *Westminster Abbey*. I meet few readers of Arnold who know it, and as Arnold's works are out of print, and the piece is not to be found in the editions of his poems contained in most libraries, it is hard to refer them to it. It is an occasional piece, but to Arnold the occasion was a great one, for it was to commemorate Arthur Stanley, Dean of Westminster; Stanley who had been the active friend of Dr. Arnold's widow and orphans, and who had written Dr. Arnold's life. The poem is a masterpiece of its kind, which may not be the highest kind of poetry. Those who seem angered at Arnold's complaint about Tennyson's lack of intellectual depth might have their eyes opened by comparing Tennyson's *Ode on the Death of Wellington* with this ode of Arnold. It was something of a feat for Arnold, now the author of *Literature and Dogma, God and the Bible, St. Paul and Protestantism*, to write on Westminster Abbey. But, though he renounces nothing of his own past doctrines, nay presses them further, the poet is singularly happy from the opening line to the last. He begins with an allusion to an old legend, known to few, but known to Stanley, about the Abbey: that on the eve of its dedication in the seventh century, St. Peter came to the opposite side of the

river and asked a fisherman to ferry him across.
While the fisherman waited to bring him back the
whole Abbey appeared illuminated with extra-
ordinary light. Then Peter returned and dis-
closed who he was. This visitation was considered
sufficient, and the dedication service which had
been planned was omitted. Nothing could have
better served the turn of Arnold, the apostle of
light, than this legend. Also the legend, which
was a favourite with the famous Dean, was well
suited to himself:

> What! for a term so scant
> Our shining visitant
> Cheer'd us, and now is pass'd into the night?
> Couldst thou no better keep, O Abbey old,
> The boon thy dedication-sign foretold,
> The presence of that gracious inmate, light?—
> A child of light appear'd;
> Hither he came, late-born and long-desired,
> And to men's hearts this ancient place endear'd;
> What, is the happy glow so soon expired?

Then the legend is poetically told and the later
history of the Abbey reviewed, glorious indeed,

> Only that primal guest the fisher saw,
> Light, only light, was slow to reappear.

> The Saviour's happy light,
> Wherein at first was dight
> His boon of life and immortality,
> In desert ice of subtleties was spent
> Or drown'd in mists of childish wonderment,

Fond fancies here, there false philosophy!
And harsh the temper grew
Of men with mind thus darken'd and astray;
And scarce the boon of life could struggle through,
For want of light which should the boon convey.

Yet in this latter time
The promise of the prime
Seem'd to come true at last, O Abbey old!
It seem'd, a child of light did bring the dower
Foreshown thee in thy consecration-hour,
And in thy courts his shining freight unroll'd;
Bright wits, and instincts sure,
And goodness warm, and truth without alloy,
And temper sweet, and love of all things pure,
And joy in light, and power to spread the joy.

Here the poet breaks off to recall, most appositely, another miracle, recorded in one of the Homeric hymns, of a human child destined for immortality, and bathed at night in flame and light by a goddess, until its mortal mother in terror intervenes and the fate is broken. The tale is woven into Stanley's troubled life and early death, but quickly we leave the lament:

And truly he who here
Hath run his bright career,
And served men nobly, and acceptance found,
And borne to light and right his witness high,
What could he better wish than then to die,
And wait the issue, sleeping underground?
Why should he pray to range
Down the long age of truth that ripens slow;

And break his heart with all the baffling change,
And all the tedious tossing to and fro?

For this and that way swings
The flux of mortal things,
Though moving inly to one far-set goal.—
What had our Arthur gain'd, to stop and see,
After light's term, a term of cecity,
A Church once large and then grown strait in soul?
To live, and see arise,
Alternating with wisdom's too short reign,
Folly revived, re-furbish'd sophistries,
And pullulating rites externe and vain?

Ay me! 'Tis deaf, that ear
Which joy'd my voice to hear;
Yet would I not disturb thee from thy tomb,
Thus sleeping in thine Abbey's friendly shade,
And the rough waves of life for ever laid!
I would not break thy rest, nor change thy doom.
Even as my father, thou—
Even as that loved, that well-recorded friend—
Hast thy commission done; ye both may now
Wait for the leaven to work, the let to end.

And thou, O Abbey grey!
Predestined to the ray
By this dear guest over thy precinct shed—
Fear not but that thy light once more shall burn,
Once more thine immemorial gleam return,
Though sunk be now this bright, this gracious head!
Let but the light appear
And thy transfigured walls be touch'd with flame—
Our Arthur will again be present here,
Again from lip to lip will pass his name.

This ode has been highly praised, likened even to Milton's ode on the Nativity. As compared with *Thyrsis* it is, of course, more occasional; indeed no one would think of calling Clough's death merely an "occasion" to Arnold; nor would Arnold ever have called Stanley, as he might have called Clough, during a period at least, *dimidium meae vitae*. Here the plangent personal note would have been out of place. Nor had the "Abbey grey" the place in Arnold's experience and affection which Oxford had. But *Westminster Abbey* is a lucid and sincere expression of one side of Arnold's thought and life, caught *musaeo lepore*. And it has a singular felicity, which would be hard to over-praise, nor is it an unfitting bow, on Matthew Arnold's "last appearance" before the public as a poet, in his sixty-first year.

I have, in these two lectures, traced Arnold's poetic career, following chronological order as well as I could, showing how that clears away some of the exaggerated statements so frequently made about his development. I propose now to say a few general things about his poetry, and, if I may venture it, offer a hint for those who have only a slight acquaintance with it.

To anyone who has read the Greek poets from Homer to Theocritus, Arnold is the most companionable English poet of his century. Indeed he takes a place among the poets who easily breathe Aegean air; who have an insight into the highly rational morality of the Greek religious teachers; and who have the Greek zest for the graciousness and joy and beauty of life. Two or three of these even share the scientific imagination which is peculiarly Greek: Lucretius, Goethe, Gray. To this smaller group Arnold does not belong. But he has the dignity and grace and austere beauty of the Greeks; their moderation, their proportion, their simplicity, their quietness, their love of elemental principles, their essential humanity. Browning, great lovable spirit as he is, and so human, lacks the discipline of the Greek; he is *continuellement égaré*, though he has genius enough to make us follow his bypaths with wonder and admiration. Landor, who spent his life in Greek studies, and who occasionally flings off a thing worthy of the Greek anthology, was somehow constitutionally unsuited to profit by his lore; he stood in his own way, perhaps lacking nobility of manhood. Wordsworth, usually described as unbookish, an untaught and irregular genius, was both by temper and by his Cambridge training fitted to range with the Greeks. His *Ode to Duty*, especially after he dropped a stanza included in the first edition, is an inspired distillation of one of the driest of Greek books—Aristotle's *Nicomachaean Ethics*. Gray, a polymath, and a penetrating Greek scholar—his notes on Plato reveal the sheerest insight—was a truncated genius, when all is said, whether through physical frailty or because born out of his time.

On Arnold, driven by need, distracted by humdrum duties, born into a materialistic and inhuman age, saddened by the early loss of half his children, the gods yet smiled. "Rigorous teachers seized" his youth, but his youth was buoyant and high-spirited. He rebelled; his life at Oxford caused many a sigh to Clough and other friends. It was a time of manifold revolt, of wasted purpose, and loss of original strength. But in Arnold there soon emerged a strength, a purpose, a high self-dedication which astonished his most intimate sister, and his older friends: so gay, indolent, and mocking he appeared. Nothing is more significant in Arnold's account of the life of the poet than his insistence on his loneliness, nor did he wish that loneliness spied out; he banned a biography. Devoted elder brother to his many brothers and sisters, a life-long stay to his long widowed mother, Arnold had an arduous life apart. Apollo had beckoned him, and thenceforward he followed, not briefly, but *sein Leben lang*, a toilsome but triumphant path.

But what shall we say to those readers of poetry who do not know the Greeks, confident in their own "unerring light". I know that for them an abundance of books and text-books are now being written about Arnold, telling them what to admire in him and why. Arnold promises to furnish a longer theme for Americans than did Dickens or Mrs. Trollope. Heaven knows how many Ph.D. theses are being written on him at this moment. Most of this stuff will not help readers to understand Arnold, nor will it very long hurt his reputation. The malice of a little soul is impotent against a great soul. *On His Own Blindness* is the proper title for the lecture of T. S. Eliot, to which I previously referred. But to return to readers of poetry who have not read Greek poetry. I have no wish to brand them in so classifying them. Certainly I have no wish to be arrogant. We are all more ignorant than learned in most fields. But I should not advise these readers, for whom a full appreciation of Arnold will be difficult, to seek help in the "hencoop of the Muses", to use the phrase they used at Athens for the scribbling annotators in Alexandria. Let them read Arnold by reading Arnold. The best commentary on any poem of Arnold is the rest of Arnold's poetry—from which, by the way, *Merope*, *Balder Dead*, and *Epilogue to Lessing's Laocoön*, may be omitted. But as I have suggested, it helps to read the poems in chronological order, and unfortunately no edition of the poems bears dates. If one must have prose notes on the poems, let them be Arnold's own prose, beginning with his first published prose, the preface to the 1853 edition of poems. These readers will presently find that despite all that has been written about Arnold's faulty ear, his poems yield great pleasure when read aloud. From the earliest poems on there are things which once read aloud become a rich part of one's experience; for example, *Mycerinus, The Forsaken Merman, Yes, in the Sea of Life Enisled.*

I interrupt myself here to give you a reminder at least of the exquisite and haunting beauty of *The Forsaken Merman*, which I have already praised so highly. (May I say in passing that I have felt obliged to quote from certain poems to make my point as I went along, and other passages at disproportionate length perhaps, because they are so little known; but that it has gone against the grain to refer so frequently to the greatest poems without allowing them to utter themselves to you):

> Come, dear children, let us away;
> Down and away below!
> Now my brothers call from the bay,
> Now the great winds shoreward blow,
> Now the salt tides seaward flow;
> Now the wild white horses play,
> Champ and chafe and toss in the spray.
> Children dear, let us away!
> This way, this way!

And so through a hundred or more lines, equally

flawless, to the marvellously beautiful close:

> But, children, at midnight,
> When soft the winds blow,
> When clear falls the moonlight,
> When spring-tides are low;
> When sweet airs come seaward
> From heaths starr'd with broom,
> And high rocks throw mildly
> On the blanch'd sands a gloom;
> Up the still, glistening beaches,
> Up the creeks we will hie,
> Over banks of bright seaweed
> The ebb-tide leaves dry.
> We will gaze, from the sand-hills,
> At the white, sleeping town;
> At the church on the hill-side—
> And then come back down,
> Singing: "There dwells a loved one,
> But cruel is she!
> She left lonely for ever
> The kings of the sea."

The poem, *Resignation*, will be more troublesome: its meaning will not deliver itself up on one reading or two. If the reader goes to the ordinary book on Arnold, and reads that the poem is inspired by Wordsworth he will be more troubled still. Rather let him put it aside until he has read more Arnold. In the next collection, whatever the reader thinks of *Empedocles* and *Tristram and Iseult*, he will again come upon great poetry which will yield a treasure on first reading: for example, *The Buried Life*, *The Future*, and many other pieces, not ignoble, will give him an insight into Arnold. After he has had that much experience of the author, I can recommend him to *The Scholar Gipsy*, even *Sohrab and Rustum*, and *Thyrsis*. On his way he will come on perfect little things to which I have made no allusion, which once read can never be forgotten. Meantime his conception of Arnold's diverse gifts will have grown. He will see that Arnold in his description of Nature is not merely Wordsworth's imitator. He writes of rivers as no one else has done. Much as he loves England, he has made Switzerland his second country. He has a passion for coolness, for the dews of morning, for shady lawns, the air of the fells and uplands and sea-beaches, for the measureless caverns of the night sky; and he describes these things in such a way as to procure for us a refreshment of spirit as well as body. For the most part he is extraordinarily lucid. Too much has been made, I think, of the difficulties in a few of his lines. I have referred to one or two of these myself. The obscurity appears the thicker, I believe, because of its contrast with the general lack of obscurity.

It is the great elemental things in man's nature which are Arnold's concern: not the mean, the petty, the trivial. Yet he does not over-simplify life, nor flatter us into believing that each of our

lives has grandeur and nobility, even though
> The same heart beats in every human breast.

He summons us rather to catch what vision we can in "hours of insight", and to resolute purpose for the sustainment of our souls in "hours of gloom". I have already remarked on Arnold's masculinity. Few women have written poetry in any age; but men often become women when they write poetry. Vergil is almost consistently so. The Greek original[1] from which Goethe took his *Über allen Gipfeln* is masculine, but in adapting it Goethe becomes-feminine.

But I forget myself! We had agreed to leave ancient literature to one side. For comparison, then, let me take Arnold and one of his contemporaries. Here is Arnold's *A Wish*:

> I ask not that my bed of death
> From bands of greedy heirs be free;
> For these besiege the latest breath
> Of fortune's favour'd sons, not me.
>
> I ask not each kind soul to keep
> Tearless, when of my death he hears.

---

[1]εὕδουσι δ' ὀρέων κορυφαί τε καὶ φάραγγες,
πρώονές τε καὶ χαράδραι,
φύλλα θ' ἑρπετά θ' ὅσσα τρέφει μέλαινα γαῖα,
θῆρες τ' ὀρεσκῷοι καὶ γένος μελισσᾶν
καὶ κνώδαλ' ἐν βένθεσσι πορφυρέας ἁλός
εὕδουσι δ' οἰωνῶν
φῦλα τανυπτερύγων—Alcman

Let those who will, if any, weep!
There are worse plagues on earth than tears.

I ask but that my death may find
The freedom to my life denied;
Ask but the folly of mankind
Then, then at last, to quit my side.

Spare me the whispering, crowded room,
The friends who come, and gape, and go;
The ceremonious air of gloom—
All, which makes death a hideous show!

Nor bring, to see me cease to live,
Some doctor full of phrase and fame,
To shake his sapient head, and give
The ill he cannot cure a name.

Nor fetch, to take the accustom'd toll
Of the poor sinner bound for death,
His brother-doctor of the soul,
To canvass with official breath

The future and its viewless things—
That undiscover'd mystery
Which one who feels death's winnowing wings
Must needs read clearer, sure, than he!

Bring none of these; but let me be,
While all around in silence lies,
Moved to the window near, and see
Once more, before my dying eyes,

Bathed in the sacred dews of morn
The wide aerial landscape spread—
The world which was ere I was born,
The world which lasts when I am dead;

> Which never was the friend of one,
> Nor promised love it could not give,
> But lit for all its generous sun,
> And lived itself, and made us live.
>
> There let me gaze, till I become
> In soul, with what I gaze on, wed!
> To feel the universe my home;
> To have before my mind—instead
>
> Of the sick room, the mortal strife,
> The turmoil for a little breath—
> The pure eternal course of life,
> Not human combatings with death!
>
> Thus feeling, gazing, might I grow
> Composed, refresh'd, ennobled, clear;
> Then willing let my spirit go
> To work or wait elsewhere or here!

Now, with that in your ears, think of Tennyson's *Crossing the Bar*.

Let me conclude on the note which Arnold preferred for his conclusions. Generally he is called a melancholy, elegiac poet. His verses so often are memorial verses and poems of frustrated love. But his poetry does animate. *The Scholar Gipsy*, so often referred to as a dirge, ends with a picture of one of the most vital and adventurous ages in the history of men. Even *Tristram and Iseult*, which I have called not one of his great poems, ends with joy attained, and with a humanization of mediaeval legend which others of the nineteenth century never caught. Sometimes the animation is given of set purpose, as in *The Last Word*, *Rugby Chapel*, *Obermann Once More*. But when Arnold is at his best, in *Sohrab and Rustum*, in *Thyrsis*, *Mycerinus*, *The Forsaken Merman*, our animation and abiding joy is the effect of the whole poem. It is a quiet, reflective joy; not the gaiety of mere animal good spirits, nor of an untroubled mental condition, but a joy neither lightly won nor lightly lost:

> A man becomes aware of his life's flow,
> And hears its winding murmur; and he sees
> The meadows where it glides, the sun, the breeze.
>
> And there arrives a lull in the hot race
> Wherein he doth for ever chase
> That flying and elusive shadow, rest.
> An air of coolness plays upon his face,
> And an unwonted calm pervades his breast.
> And then he thinks he knows
> The hills where his life rose,
> And the sea where it goes.

IV

ARNOLD THE CRITIC AND PROSE WRITER

THOSE who have Arnold's works complete, or nearly complete, on their shelves—a difficult achievement nowadays—know what a voluminous writer he was. The purpose of these lectures precludes, I have come to believe, that I should do more than allude to his writings on religion, or to his educational reports. This is a pity in a way, for religion and education are to most of us, or should be, deeply interesting subjects; and again it is impossible to deal piecemeal with Arnold's work, in any completely satisfactory way. He was only twenty-eight when he became a school inspector, and held the post thirty-five years. The work, though at first uncongenial to him, became in time a large part of his life. Quite early he saw that it would enable him to do some things on which he had already set his heart. As to religion, though I have shown, I hope, that it did not become a preoccupation of his so soon as did political, and more particularly social, questions, yet from the outset Arnold was a deeply religious man and continued to be so all his life. Also one can see at least as early as the poem, *Resignation*, published when he was only twenty-six, that his religious ideas are presently not going to be orthodox. The Greeks, even the comic poet, Aristophanes, never attempted to write of life leaving such themes as education and religion to one side. And the Greeks were Arnold's models. Still, I believe that these Alexander Lectures are, in intention, limited to literature as most of us conceive literature, and that even in dealing with Matthew Arnold, for whom poetry was a "criticism of life" in the widest and deepest sense, and who despite ironical allusions to himself as a *belles-lettrist*, hated to be considered a merely "literary gentleman" or have his work considered as "mere literature", we must confine ourselves to his poetry and his "literary" criticism in prose.

His first published work in prose was the Preface to his 1853 edition of poems. Arnold was then thirty years old. In considering his prose works, as in considering his poetry, it is of some importance to date the work. Just observe how much of the commonly accepted account of Arnold's development the dating of this essay sweeps away. We are commonly asked to believe that Arnold early in life devoted himself entirely to "poetry" pure and simple; but that in middle life, having become a school inspector, and being distracted by these duties, his poetic inspiration dried up, and that he took to writing prose, first about literature, later about politics and social questions, of which he knew very little, and later still about religion and theology of which he knew less. I do not say that all these mistakes are precisely set down, but that is something like the general inference a reader gathers from Saintsbury and from Paul, who wrote the account of Arnold in the *English Men of Letters* series. These men set the fashion, just about the turn of the century, and it has not been easy, in the absence of a biography, and in the absence of a dated edition of the poems, for later writers to escape the old errors. The highly censored edition of Arnold's *Letters*, which G. W. E. Russell published in 1895, should have prevented Saintsbury, writing in 1899, and Paul, writing in 1902, from making some of their blunders. But Paul shared Gladstone's antipathy to Arnold, and the learned and vivacious Professor Saintsbury could hardly escape a tendency to score off a reputation now grown so great as Matthew Arnold's.

It is worth while, even at the expense of some repetition and recapitulation to observe certain things at this point. The earliest poem, aside from the boyish prize poems, which we can date with certainty, is the sonnet on Shakespeare, 1844. Arnold was not twenty-two until December 24 of that year. As has been remarked by others in recent years, this sonnet is surely as much to be called criticism as any of the later prose works. The critical bent, then, existed in Arnold from the very beginning. Politics and social questions shape clear in the poems which followed in the next few years. Indeed they had already loomed vaguely in the prize poems at Rugby and Oxford, and in the poem, *Mycerinus*, which I am inclined to place soon after the prize poems. Before Arnold was twenty-five he was writing prose criticism, not altogether immature as criticism, though very much so in the style of the prose, in letters to Clough, touching on George Sand, Tennyson, Milton, and Clough's own work. At the same age he was already initiated into politics, in a certain sense of the term, through being secretary to Lord Lansdowne. Now, at the age of thirty, we find him publishing a prose work of criticism, in which some of his most permanent critical principles are already embodied. Not for another thirteen or fourteen years is he to finish *Thyrsis*, which may be considered his finest poem. When writing *Thyrsis* he had been a school inspector fifteen years.

The sequence of things in Arnold's development is now coming to be better appreciated and understood, partly through scholars on this side of the Atlantic, including the critical work of a professor in this University. But even one of these scholars,[1] to whose work I am indebted,

---

[1] Professor H. F. Lowry, editor, *Letters of M. Arnold to A. H. Clough* (1932).

laments that Arnold gave up poetry for political wrangling; hints that admiration for Sainte-Beuve had something to do with Arnold's turning to criticism; and wishes that we had more poetry from him and less about the Philistines. I think that this sort of lament is idle about any genius, but particularly about Arnold, who had in him early the seeds of what he was later to be; who wished from the beginning to see life steadily and see it whole; and, who, like his father, so admired those Periclean Athenians, who were in the same person generals and historians and mining contractors; common soldiers and sculptors and philosophers, and who were all active politicians, jurymen in the law courts, annual judges of literature, and regular participants in religious festivals.

Early, early in life Arnold resolved not to live in a study, but to be a disseminator of ideas. Now if such a statement were overheard by Lytton Strachey, or other unintelligent critics of Arnold, they would say: "Precisely! That is what I have said of Arnold. Poetry with Arnold was not poetry at all, only a means to an end. This statement you have made condemns him as a poet, and as a critic."

Let us look into this. Let us go back to a period more than four years earlier than the 1853 Preface, to a letter written to Clough early in the year 1849. (Clough has just published some poems):

My dear Clough,
 If I were to say the real truth as to your poems in general, as they impress me—it would be this—that they are not *natural*. Many persons with far lower gifts than yours yet seem to find their natural mode of expression in poetry, and tho: the contents may not be very valuable they appeal with justice from the judgement of the mere thinker to the world's general appreciation of naturalness—i.e.—an absolute propriety—of form, as the sole *necessary* of Poetry as such: whereas the greatest wealth and depth of matter is merely a superfluity in the Poet *as such*.

—Form of Conception comes by nature certainly, but is generally developed late; but this lower form, of expression, is found from the beginning amongst all born poets, even feeble thinkers, and in an unpoetical age: as Collins, Greene and fifty more, in England only.

The question is not of congruity between conception and expression: which when both are poetical, is the poet's highest result:—you say what you mean to say: but in such a way as to leave it doubtful whether your mode of expression is not quite arbitrarily adopted.

I often think that even a slight gift of poetical expression which in a common person might have developed itself easily and naturally, is overlaid and crushed in a profound thinker so as to be of no use to him to help him to express himself.—The trying to go into and to the bottom of an object instead of grouping *objects* is as fatal to the sensuousness of poetry as the mere painting, (for, *in Poetry*, this is not *grouping*) is to its airy and rapidly moving life.

"Not deep the Poet sees, but wide" [a quotation from *Resignation*, let me interpolate]:—think of this as you gaze from the Cumner Hill toward Cirencester and Cheltenham.

—You succeed best you see, in fact, in the hymn, where man, his deepest personal feelings being in play, finds poetical expression as *man* only, not as artist:—but consider whether you attain the *beautiful*, and whether your product gives PLEASURE, not excites curiosity and reflexion. Forgive all this: but I am always prepared myself to give up the attempt, on conviction: and so, I know, are you: and I only urge you to reflect whether you are advancing. Reflect too, as I cannot but do here more and more, in spite of all the nonsense some people talk, how deeply *unpoetical* the age and all one's surroundings are. Not unprofound, not ungrand, not unmoving:—but *unpoetical*.
Ever yrs.
M. A.

This truly extraordinary letter was written just on the eve of the publication of Matthew Arnold's first collection of poems—a collection which he did not sign. It is not an easy letter to understand, even when read in connection with the poem, *Resignation*, as Professor Lowry advises. Not for years after this was Arnold to find prose composition easy. But on close attention the letter has an unmistakable meaning. "Form of Conception", that is, poetry in its major sense, "comes by Nature, certainly". That is to say there can be no question but that it is inspired. But the inspiration takes greater and lesser shape in different men. Some have the gift of expression, others again are too much thinkers, which crushes poetical expression. It is only when both things are in perfect balance that we have "the poet's highest result". And how can the poet tell whether he has succeeded? There are two tests: first, whether his work is beautiful to contemplate; second, whether it gives pleasure, instead of merely causing the reader to think. And at this time, before he has published anything, and more than four years before he signs his work, he announces that he is ready to give up poetry if he can convince himself, on such tests, that he is not attaining perfection. We must remember, of course, that this high statement, about the poet's belief in his inspiration as a great poet, is confided only to his most intimate friend.

Let us come to grips now with the 1853 Preface. It begins with an explanation of *Empedocles on Etna* being omitted from the present edition, and abruptly asks what poetry is. It is imitation or representation and gives a natural pleasure, as Aristotle said. But while any accurate representation may be "interesting", "more than this is demanded" from poetical works:

It is demanded, not only that it shall interest, but also that it shall inspirit and rejoice the reader: that it shall convey a charm, and infuse delight. For the Muses, as Hesiod says, were born that they might be "a forgetfulness of evils, and a truce from cares": and it is not enough that the Poet should add to the knowledge of men, it is required of him also that he should add to their happiness. "All Art", says Schiller, "is dedicated to Joy, and there is no higher and no more serious problem, than how to make men happy. The right Art is that alone, which creates the highest enjoyment."

Now, though tragedy, too, is a form of art, and the more tragic the situation the deeper the form of enjoyment, there are situations from which,
> no poetical enjoyment can be derived. They are those in which the suffering finds no vent in action; in which a continuous state of mental distress is prolonged, unrelieved by incident, hope, or resistance. . . .
> To this class of situations, . . . that of Empedocles, as I have endeavoured to represent him, belongs.

He modestly asks why he should recount all this about not reprinting a poem of his own. It is because he does not wish it to be thought that he bows to a current opinion that contemporary poets "must leave the exhausted past". This is false doctrine.
> What are the eternal objects of Poetry, among all nations, and at all times? They are actions;

human actions; possessing an inherent interest in themselves, and which are to be communicated in an interesting manner by the art of the Poet. Vainly will the latter imagine that he has everything in his own power; that he can make an intrinsically inferior action equally delightful with a more excellent one by his treatment of it: he may indeed compel us to admire his skill, but his work will possess, within itself, an incurable defect.

The Poet, then, has in the first place to select an excellent action; and what actions are the most excellent? Those, certainly, which most powerfully appeal to the great primary human affections: to those elementary feelings which subsist permanently in the race, and which are independent of time. These feelings are permanent and the same; that which interests them is permanent and the same also. The modernness or antiquity of an action, therefore, has nothing to do with its fitness for poetical representation.

Further, it is beside the mark to say that a modern poet cannot, because of his ignorance, treat a great action of the past: He may not know all the circumstances of the lives of Oedipus or Macbeth, the poet's "business is with their inward man", and this is as "accessible to a modern Poet as to a contemporary".

The action, its selection and construction, "the Greeks understood far more clearly than we do". The action and its conduct by the poet was their first consideration: "with us attention is mainly fixed on . . . the separate thoughts and images. They regarded the whole; we regard the parts. . . . Not that they failed in expression . . ., they are the highest models of expression, the unapproached masters of the *grand style*: but their expression is so excellent because it is so admirably kept in its right degree of prominence."

> For all kinds of poetry alike there was one point on which they [the Greeks] were rigidly exacting; the adaptability of the subject to the kind of poetry selected, and the careful construction of the poem.
>
> How different a way of thinking from this is ours! . . . We have critics who seem to direct their attention merely to detached expressions, ... They will permit the Poet to select any action he pleases, . . . provided he gratifies them with occasional bursts of fine writing.

He next proceeds to criticize *Faust* on this high basis, though he admits the author of it to be "the greatest poet of modern times, the greatest critic of all times".

What of English writers? At present they have no real guide, and must therefore fix their attention on excellent models. Shakespeare will first be thought of: "the greatest of all poetical names". Shakespeare knew how to choose excellent actions, nor did he limit himself to contemporary actions; furthermore he knew how to construct architecturally. But he had in addition to this an unrivalled gift of expression, abundant and irresistibly striking, and the mischief is that, this gift being so much easier to see and recognize, so many of our poets have fixed upon that exclusively for imitation. As an example Arnold takes a poem of Keats. The action in *Isabella* is carelessly treated, whereas "this one short poem contains, perhaps, a greater number of happy single expressions than all the extant tragedies of Sophocles". He praises Hallam for having the courage, in a time when Shakespeare was blindly idolized, to point out how faulty, difficult, and tortured Shakespeare's language often is. Perhaps his audience partly accounted for Shakespeare's lack of self-restraint. (Here, let me interpolate, is a hint of the great kingdom the critic has.) In his far richer thought Shakespeare rises above the ancients; "in his strong conception of his subject", in the "way in which he is penetrated with it, he resembles them, and is unlike the moderns: but in the accurate limitation of it, the conscientious rejection of superfluities, the simple and rigorous development of it from the first line of his work to the last, he falls below them, and comes nearer to the moderns. . . . He is therefore a less safe model."

> The present age makes great claims upon us: we owe it service, it will not be satisfied without our admiration. I know not how it is, but their com-

merce with the ancients appears to me to produce, in those who constantly practise it, a steadying and composing effect upon their judgment, not of literary work only, but of men and events in general. They are like persons who have had a very weighty and impressive experience: they are more truly than others under the empire of facts, and more independent of the language current among those with whom they live. They wish neither to applaud nor to revile their age; they wish to know what it is, what it can give them, and whether this is what they want. What they want, they know very well; they want to educe and cultivate what is best and noblest in themselves: they know, too, that this is no easy task.

After this high doctrine Arnold again drops to a modest disclaimer about himself:

> I am far indeed from making any claim, for myself, that I possess this discipline; or for the following Poems, that they breathe its spirit. But I say, that in the sincere endeavour to learn and practise, amid the bewildering confusion of our times, what is sound and true in poetical art, I seemed to myself to find the only sure guidance, the only solid footing, among the ancients.

This essay, Arnold's first prose publication, bears re-reading and study to-day, familiar as quotation has made it to many of us. In 1853 it was extraordinarily novel and striking. Not since Wordsworth and Coleridge had criticism taken so high a line, seldom had any English critic made such a sweep. It is obvious that he hardly hopes to carry conviction with all his readers; yet there is a quiet assurance in the tone—not the browbeating assurance of Macaulay and the earlier school of Edinburgh reviewers. The modesty is also quiet, neither apologetic nor ingratiating. What makes both assurance and modesty so convincing is that he is so sure of his principles that he has first of all turned them against himself, and rejected the very titlepiece of his last edition: this is a criticism *capable de tout*. We have seen that four years earlier he has privately expressed the resolve to give up poetry altogether if he can convince himself that he is falling below the "highest poetic result".

But, aside from the novelty of tone and the desire to come at truth, at whatever cost to himself, there is a sureness of critical touch and a ripe wisdom in this essay which makes it a landmark. Modern West Europeans had been writing about the Greeks for about three hundred years, and the Romans had pondered them for a similar period. No Greek scholar could have been surprised at what Arnold here says about the Greeks, and yet no one, so far as I remember, had put the matter in quite this way before, certainly no one had been so lucid about it. But to connect all this with a criticism of Shakespeare and contemporary English poets; with allusions to French and German criticism, not with any parade of his reading, as had been customary with Macaulay and others; and above all to be so sound and soberly judicial, not to apply adjectives to an author, but in something of Aristotle's manner to put his hand on the matter in question and invite his reader to consider it with him—this was something new in English criticism.

To say, however, as Mr. Paul said, that this was Arnold's best prose, and to suggest that his later prose fell away from this high mark, is silly and uncritical. It is Arnold's first prose writing, of any length; as we saw in an earlier lecture it gave him infinite pains to compose. After more practice he became more at home with his vehicle. It is good writing, but it is not deft or easy, nor do I detect in it any hint of that irony which Arnold's later prose so delicately exhibits.

The Preface contains a sentence, read above, which is not carefully read by some of Arnold's critics: the sentence describing those tragic situations from which no poetical enjoyment can be derived. "They are those in which the suffering finds no vent in action, in which a continuous state of mental distress is prolonged, unrelieved by incident, hope or resistance." Some have said that if this condemns *Empedocles* it condemns nearly all of Arnold's work. Those who say this have overlooked Arnold's culminating word, *resistance*.

I have touched on this in discussing *The Scholar Gipsy*. The same applies to *Thyrsis*, to *Resignation*, to *Obermann Once More*, to *Stanzas from the Grande Chartreuse*; it is the inspiring note in such an otherwise elegiac and mournful piece as *Rugby Chapel*; it is the contrapuntal theme in *Dover Beach*; it is very striking in that brief dirge, *The Last Word*, and in the passionate Marguerite poems: how little his grief when seen

>   In the stir of the forces
>   Whence issued the world!

What "resistance" in

>   Made my tost heart its very life-blood spill,
>   Yet could not break it!

One could bring out this point in many other poems.

Now, in this going back for a moment to the poetry I am not straying from my theme, which at present is Arnold's prose criticism. My point is that if Arnold were so foolish as to reject *Empedocles* on a ground on which he could just as well have rejected all his other poetry he would be no critic at all. Some have said, with little less than a sneer, that after all this parade he did later republish *Empedocles*. Yes, he did listen to the importunity of Browning and others, and republish it. But he had made his point about it, he had branded it as a failure on the whole, and he stood by that. If the world wished it for the lyrics, which he knew were lovely, let them have it. And now, at the conclusion of this examination of Arnold's first and very brief essay in prose, let us look at the order of his development, for a moment or two, again. He neither gave up attention to poetry in this year, nor did he immediately begin to write more prose. In the following year a second edition of the poems was called for. He busied himself in revising, rejecting previous poems, and adding a new one. In 1855, he brought out "Poems: A New Series", which contained as new poems, *Balder Dead* and *Separation*. In 1857 another edition appeared, this containing as a novelty the beautiful poem, *Yes, in the Sea of Life Enisled*. The same year he was appointed Professor of Poetry in Oxford, but seems to have concerned himself far less with the lectures than with the play, *Merope*, which he said he regarded as his real inauguration, and with some other poems which he wrote in Switzerland. During 1858 he is still much taken up with *Merope*. During 1859 he wrote at least two poems, *A Southern Night* and *Stanzas from Carnac*, as well as a pamphlet on Italy and a Report on European Schools. It was in 1860-61 that Arnold next occupied himself in any serious way with writing prose; the Lectures on Homer. This was seven to eight years after his first short prose publication. With these Lectures on Homer we shall now proceed to deal. For most North Americans nowadays, Arnold's *Lectures on Translating Homer* are remote in interest, and so, though they are immensely congenial to me, I deem it wise to shorten sail. The lectures altogether form a little book. I attempt only a brief sketch of them, sufficient I hope to fit them into his development as a prose critic. They constitute Arnold's first ambitious work in prose (aet. 38-39). To the ordinary reader they must often sound a little dogmatic. But Arnold had to sweep away much silly fanciful comment on Homer: impatience is indicated in the very motto of the work: *Nunquamne reponam?* He is brusque at the beginning with a sentimental criticism by Ruskin, and with the poet Cowper's sheer inability to understand Homer's style or merit. To the unfortunate Professor Newman and his translation, Arnold seems at times almost brutal, but it is fair to remember that the professor had, despite his erudition in many fields, given deep offence to a lover of Homer, calling him "quaint, garrulous, prosaic, low", and had throughout shown a total lack of appreciation of poetry while undertaking to translate the greatest of poetry. There are a few slips, perhaps, through over-vehemence about Mr. Newman, an exaggerated remark about some lines of Tennyson, two of the suggested examples of hexameters are unfortunate, though not, I think, Arnold's long hexameter specimen, which is highly successful and suggests Homer's lofty manner very well. Newman, with his great philological learning, and considerable eloquence, is easily able to retort on some of these over-vehement remarks and to complain of some of the hexameters, but not in such a way as to show that he has any poetic or critical taste, or ability to translate Homer. One wishes Arnold had shown the moderation, customary to him later, in criticizing Newman and Tennyson.

But I must not stop over these things in the space at my disposal. Rather I wish to show that in this first considerable prose work of criticism Arnold displays at almost every turn sheer critical power. The slips I have mentioned are not, at any rate, lapses from critical ability. He characterizes Homer in several ways: he is simple, direct, rapid, flowing, and in the grand style; then by quoting him he shows what he means, and, by quoting his translators from Chapman on, he shows how one or another of them has caught one of these qualities or more, but missed others. The grand style he illustrates from Vergil, Dante, and Milton, as well as from Homer himself.

As to his criticism of Homer, perhaps I cannot do better than quote from a lecture delivered by the late A. E. Housman in 1892:

Who are the great critics of the classical literatures, . . . the critics who teach with authority and not as the scribes? They are such men as Lessing or Goethe or Matthew Arnold, scholars no doubt, but not scholars of minute or profound learning. Matthew Arnold went to his grave under the impression . . . that the words ἀνδρὸς παιδοφόνοιο ποτὶ στόμα χεῖρ' ὀρέγεσθαι meant "to carry to my lips the hand of him that slew my son". We pedants know better: . . . the verse of Homer really means "to reach forth my hand to the chin of him who slew my son". But when it comes to literary criticism, heap up in one scale all the literary criticism that the whole nation of professed scholars ever wrote, and drop into the other the thin green volume of Matthew Arnold's *Lectures on Translating Homer*, which has long been out of print because the British public does not care to read it, and the first scale, as Milton says, will straight fly up and kick the beam.

It is worth remembering too, at least it is worth the classical scholars' while to remember—there are perhaps as many of them here in Toronto as in any place on this continent—that Arnold wrote in the days when forty theories were being offered about Homer, and the old Wolfian doctrine was still resounding. Arnold's purely literary criticism of Homer did much to make men feel that most of the German account of the origin of Homer was fantastic, and that, however wide and diverse the origins of epic were, *one* great poetic mind had shaped the *Iliad*.

It is not merely about Homer, however, that Arnold's touch is sure. In a hundred and one allusions to English poetry, early and late, to early French and German poetry, to Dante and Vergil, Arnold shows an almost unerring critical power. Not only had there been nothing like it in English criticism before: there has been nothing so catholic and penetrating since. In a dozen books, and many more articles, one may read nowadays that Arnold was not an exhaustive scholar, that he did not follow the all-devouring historical method of criticism, and so forth. And it is true that against some of his most sweeping generalizations minor exceptions may be made. But what should be remembered is that they are minor exceptions. Arnold deliberately limited himself if not to the greatest things in literature, at least to those things which for one reason or another have some mark of genius about them; and to leading tendencies, not to minor currents and eddies. Dozens, seemingly, of little experts are now ready to spring up and lecture Arnold's ghost on points about ballad poetry, or the early French romances. I myself know many men who know things about Homer and Homeric times of which Arnold never dreamed. But any of these points is as trivial as a barnacle on a ship. Arnold was concerning himself with certain failures of translators of Homer, which sprang from their lack of critical appreciation of

Homer's poetry. This led him on to give his own appreciation of Homer, and so to illustrate by comparison with other great literature, and lesser literature.

I, for one, do not regret that Arnold's first great work in criticism was on a subject of which perhaps few in this audience, and perhaps not more than two or three hundred persons on this continent, know anything. Homer I believe to be one of the two great poets of all time. If Arnold was to wield an influence as a critic, if he was to shape English poetry and English criticism as he obviously, in his 1853 Preface, hoped to do, it was with the greatest poetry in the world that he must begin. Our present West European civilization may die before Arnold's effect on English poetry and English criticism can be felt. But Homer has lived through the fall of several civilizations, and will probably outlive the coming dark ages, as will parts of English literature. In that case, Arnold's *Lectures on Translating Homer* perhaps stand as good a chance of affecting the future as Aristotle's *Poetics*.

But, someone may object, why drag all this in about the rise and fall of civilization! We are talking surely about literature! I reply that in a discussion of Matthew Arnold what I have said just now is absolutely relevant. It is one of Arnold's greatnesses that he foresaw the disintegration in which we are now living, the end of which is not yet. But many of his critics, confident that their academic and journalistic positions will be everlasting, and deeply annoyed because Arnold, of whom they undertake to write—as they will undertake anything—was complex, versatile, rooted in the past and provident of the future, complain that he did not stick to his job of writing poetry, and evidently think that if he did criticize he should at least have confined himself to academic and journalistic lines, as did Saintsbury and the other writers of text-books, and as do a host of ignoble, wit-snapping penny-a-liners to-day. Something of the kind doubtless, while the lives and activities of men flowed on to disaster, was retorted to the Hebrew prophets and to Thucydides.

V

ARNOLD THE CRITIC AND PROSE WRITER
(continued)

WE move on now to the period 1861-65, Arnold's late thirties and early forties; the period marked first of all by the death of Clough, 1861, and the musings which led up to the composition of *Thyrsis*, 1866. It is, therefore, despite all that can be said on the *slimness* of Arnold's poetic output, a most important poetic period for him: certainly it cannot be said that he was now playing on "scrannel pipes". But, from 1861 on, Arnold was musing upon other things as well: first, the vehemence of the outbursts on his *Lectures on Translating Homer*, which indicated to him, more clearly than ever, the obliquity of vision to be found even in men of learning, for lack of any body of critical opinion; second, the complacency of public men about the unlovely, and cruelly unjust, social framework of England; third, the condition of religion in England. Many writers have seen the great importance of Arnold's *Essays in Criticism*, published 1865, both intrinsically and as a landmark in Arnold's life. Many critics have declared that *Thyrsis*, published 1867, is the finest of Arnold's poetry, and one of the great things in all English poetry. But, seemingly, few of these writers think it worth while to remember that these two elements in Arnold's genius were germinating and flowering together; and certainly the common statement is that poetry came first with Matthew Arnold, then prose: that he was creative first and critical afterwards; that he gave up literature for social and religious writing. Such statements, which are almost entirely false, are constantly iterated; as they still stand in the way of a true appreciation of Arnold's endowment, his character and genius, I keep asking, perhaps with some tedium to you, that you take another view of his development.

By 1862, if we may, as I think we safely can, leave aside minor things—private letters, technical educational reports, a pamphlet on Italy—we can say that Arnold has written two important bits of prose: the 1853 Preface and the Homer lectures, 1861-62. The first, though it looks forward to so much in Arnold, is a brief parergon, incidental to his own poetry. The second, by no means brief, arises directly from his own poetic studies, from *Sohrab and Rustum*, if you will. But it carries him over a wide field, indeed it is a sketch (though Arnold's modesty would have forbidden him to call it such) of the great poetry of Europe, from Homer on. With his own poetic inspiration still undimmed; with his training, especially the incessant study which Arnold had been making since early manhood of great poets and thinkers and periods—Homer, the Periclean Age, Sophocles, Plato, Lucretius, the Bible, Dante, the Renascence and the Reformation, Shakespeare, Goethe, French civilization, Wordsworth—with all these testimonials to human greatness and grandeur ever in his mind, Arnold surveyed the contemporary English scene and tried to understand it, its etiology and implications. The picture of him at this period, which the wilful critics draw of him: an "elegant literary gentleman" who had published "a few slim volumes of verse", the "incumbent of the Oxford Chair of Poetry", a man of "narrow training", "limited to a narrow though cultured circle" (these phrases which I string together are quotations) is utterly fantastic.[1] For his day

---

[1] It is truly astonishing how this wilful and unconsidered writing about Arnold still continues. Some of you have no doubt been reading the reminiscences of Mr. Logan Pearsall Smith in the last three numbers of the *Atlantic Monthly*. Mr. Smith is engagingly frank about the crudity of his own youthful judgments, but now in old age he apparently does not think that his youthful judgment of Arnold needs revision or qualification. It is interesting to observe that what impressed him most was *Culture and Anarchy*. His views are similar to some of those which I have been at pains to controvert. More than half a century ago he met Arnold in Dresden, and thought him a mere snob. He wondered how this man could have been the author of works he had read with such admiration. One could forgive youth the inadequacy of such a judgment. But now, in his seventies, with his reputation as a critic in other fields established, Mr. Smith harks back to his youthful bewilderment: Arnold was nothing but a snob, his literary work is a mystery.

Matthew Arnold was widely travelled: he was almost as much at home in Paris as in London; his judgments on the confusing scene in Europe and America were no more astray than Mr. Gladstone's, or than those of other English public men; at any rate they did not spring from aloofness from the public scene; for more than ten years he had moved, in a minor way, in politics and the civil service; during a decade as marshall on a judge's circuit, and as school inspector he had travelled the length and breadth of England, with opportunities, therefore, of a special kind to see into all manner of cross-sections of English society. With great native endowment of sympathy, with a divine gift of imagination, with a discipline broad and at many points deep, and having as a routine daily task to examine those institutions of a community which are the surest index to its social and intellectual well-being, and comparing these with similar institutions in several countries of the Continent, Arnold was really in a unique position to see life steadily and see it whole. This was the man, in the period I have described, who took up his pen on *The Function of Criticism at the Present Time.* The title is worth observing. As we have seen Arnold consciously addressed himself to his contemporaries. But one may see the universal in the particular: this essay, local and topical and temporal in its references, has an enduring value.

The essay is prefaced[2] by certain modest allusions to the lectures on Homer; sneers at his Oxford professorship elicit from him a highly poetical description of Oxford; and then follows a quotation of the definition of criticism he had given in the Oxford lectures: "in all branches of knowledge, theology, philosophy, history, art, science, to see the object as in itself it really is". But, as if to anticipate a chorus of objections: "How can any one be sure that he really does this!" Arnold had approached the matter with soft words:

> To try and approach Truth on one side after another, not to strive or cry, not to persist in pressing forward, on any one side, with violence and self-will,—it is only thus, it seems to me, that mortals may hope to gain any vision of the mysterious Goddess, whom we shall never see except in outline, but only thus even in outline.

It is like the tentative, groping way in which Aristotle approaches a subject. And, after his definition, he expands and illustrates it, first from literature then from politics and society. Criticism "tends to establish an order of ideas, if not absolutely true, yet true by comparison with that which it displaces; . . . Presently these new ideas reach society, the touch of truth is the touch of life, and there is a stir and growth everywhere;

---

[2]This Preface is not reprinted in all editions.

out of this stir and growth come the creative epochs of literature." He alludes to Periclean Athens, Elizabethan England, Goethe's Germany. Then, *via* an allusion to the French Revolution, he glides into politics, the writings of Burke, who had brought thought into politics; and, after quoting the recent saying of a member of Parliament, that "it was no objection to a thing that it was an anomaly", he generalizes on the aloofness of current English politics from thought and intelligence. Without pressing this too hard, for a moment, he comments on the bad sense in which the word, *curiosity*, is generally used in English. In other languages it means a disinterested free play of the mind on all subjects, for its own sake. But real criticism is essentially just this! Here, then, is a tentative second definition of criticism.

The mention of the French wars suggests that England has long been at peace; European ideas ought, therefore, to "steal gradually and amicably in, and mingle, . . . with our own notions". Englishmen have had a long money-making period, too, and hence have leisure; they travel, they are sure of their own practice and conduct, and need not fear to entertain one or two novelties of thought. This is subtly done.

Another subtlety follows. Assuming that English criticism is already in existence, Arnold blandly goes on to say that it will want in its progress a rule for guidance: this is disinterestedness. Its business will be, as it knows the best that has been known and thought in the world, to create new ideas. Insinuating by his method of statement, that Englishmen are anxious to embark on this voyage, and that it is not "an idea that has crawled up his ain back", Arnold then makes a deadly contrast: across the Channel the *Revue des deux mondes*, in Britain the *Whig Review*, the *Tory Review*, the *Dissenters' Review*, the *Catholic Review*. Till recently there had been an excellent *Home and Foreign Review*: it had died for lack of support. Burke's "living by ideas" had been referred to. Now two public men of the present day are cited: one claiming that the Anglo-Saxon breed is "superior to all the world", the other praying "that our unrivalled happiness may last". Moralizing a little, quoting from Goethe, and partially excusing such "dithyrambs" by reference to the controversies of English public life, Arnold then sets down a newspaper item, printed just below the second politician's speech:

> A shocking child-murder has just been committed at Nottingham. A girl named Wragg left the workhouse there on Saturday morning with her young illegitimate child. The child was soon afterwards found dead on Mapperly Hills, having been strangled. Wragg is in custody.

Arnold now chants a strain of his own, using the

CRITIC AND PROSE WRITER 129

phrases, "our unrivalled happiness", "our Anglo-Saxon breed", and "Wragg is in custody", for refrains. Then, admitting that his method may be thought "subtle and indirect", and this sort of criticism "slow and obscure", he roundly declares:

> But it is the only proper work of criticism. The mass of mankind will never have any ardent zeal for seeing things as they are; . . . whoever sets himself to see things as they are will find himself one of a very small circle; but it is only by this small circle resolutely doing its own work that adequate ideas will ever get current . . . only by remaining collected, and refusing to lend himself to the point of view of the practical man, can the critic do the practical man any service.

Once more he pushes into political and religious matters—into the latter at considerable length—and thereafter, insisting that he is guilty of no digression, returns to literature briefly, before the essay closes.

I am content to let this essay on *The Function of Criticism at the Present Time* speak for itself through these short extracts.

But it was not enough to proclaim the greatness of the critic and the need for real criticism in England of the day. Arnold follows with essays at once provocative and ingratiating, abounding in information for most of his readers, and arresting, both in matter and style. The phrases do not glitter so much as stimulate, occasionally they sting. The first is a chapter on *The Literary Influence of Academies.* There is plenty of evidence, here and in his other writings, that Arnold knew his countrymen too well to imagine that they would ever establish or submit to an institution like the French Academy. He knows, too, that the French Academy has not always been on the side of the angels. But he seizes the publication of a history of that institution as an opportunity to tell something about its purposes, so that he may have a background, a foil, for examples of provincialism and bad taste in English literature, early and late.

In this collection are the two essays on the brother and sister de Guérin. One does not feel that they are being exhibited as great figures in French literature. Rather, they are represented as slight figures, but attractive; the brother with a gift for poetic prose. But, again, they provide a background for *aperçus* on English literature; they enable Arnold to transport his readers across the Channel, and to throw off casual remarks on George Sand and Sainte-Beuve, ironically assuming that all English readers would be well acquainted with these at least; they introduce remarks on French Catholicism and English Protestantism, and then on the memoirs of a young Englishwoman, Miss Emma Tatham, who sang "in a sweet low voice" at Hawley-Square Chapel:

My Jesus to know, and feel his blood flow,
'Tis life everlasting, 'tis heaven below.

Eugénie de Guérin, on the other hand, though a Catholic, thought the lives of the Saints "dangerous reading", especially for young girls:—"What one reads has such power over one's feelings; and these, even in seeking God, sometimes go astray."

Many readers, I think, certainly several critics of Arnold, miss the subtle purpose of these two essays, miss the delicate irony of their method; and ask why Arnold, who talks so much of the grand style, and the high function of the critic, wastes his time on such slight figures as the de Guérins. Yet Arnold had warned his readers, in the introductory essay of the collection, how roundly the critic must go to work.

There follows the delicious essay on *Heinrich Heine*. Arnold records in a letter how irresistible were some of the quotations from Heine when this piece was given as a lecture. (The essay should be read in conjunction with Arnold's poem on Heinrich Heine's grave.) It will at once be observed that Arnold feels he has here got hold of a vastly greater figure than the de Guérins, and before he is through he gives us a serious review of Heine's greatness and his limitations: indeed is there anywhere a more delicately balanced estimate of all the aspects of Heine? At any rate it is serious criticism "for its own sake". And yet we feel, too, that Arnold is using his opportunity to deal with Heine for an immediate purpose in relation to his group of essays. He carries his readers not only to Paris, with Heine, but to Germany. The subject enables him to cite weightily, as he always does, the criticisms of Goethe on poetry and life. Again, to deal with Heine is to plunge into a *mélange* of poetry, religion, and politics. But, as if to brim the measure full with opportunities for Arnold, Heine had also been to England and wittily criticized the English. So it was in this essay that Arnold first expounded the modern meaning of the word, Philistine.

The following chapter, on *Pagan and Mediaeval Religious Sentiment*, most people know. Far from thinking this is Arnold at his best, as some suggest, I do not even think it a characteristic piece. It is not even well considered, nor artistically rounded out, though that part which is a translation from Theocritus is carefully done, and obviously gave its author satisfaction. But there is not the slightest subtlety in the contrast between Theocritus and St. Francis, nor was the contrast worth instituting. This essay, so much praised, illustrates what I have once or twice alluded to: his lack, on many occasions, of real historic sense. In his opening remarks he speaks of Catholicism as though it were all of a piece, from the establishment of the Roman bishopric to his own day.

CRITIC AND PROSE WRITER 133

Later he speaks of "pagan times" as though Greeks and Romans had anything in common, as though the Greek and Roman civilizations together made a unit, as though the Greeks themselves had not a long development. (Of course this fatuous idea of a Greco-Roman civilization occurs in a thousand books, and is not Arnold's peculiar error.) One would not gather that the scene of the poem he translates was Egypt, ruled over by Macedonians, who had conquered the Greeks, and were now exploiting them to glorify a mongrel empire. The piece is, however, a mere *jeu d'esprit*, a by-product of Arnold's study of Theocritus.

The essay which follows, *A Persian Passion Play*, to which few have paid attention, is similarly, no doubt, a by-product of his reading of Persian history at an earlier period. To me it seems no more satisfactory as an illumination or comment on the play at Ammergau, than is the preceding essay a commentary on Greek religion.

Once more Arnold picks on an obscure French writer, *Joubert*, as a text, and in this essay he tells us precisely why he has done so. Such men, he says, are "capable of emitting a life-giving stimulus". A very stimulating essay this remains: informative of the France of Joubert's period (1754-1824); but also the subject permits a comparison with Coleridge; gives Joubert's opinions on Voltaire; his allusions to Buffon and others; his views on religion, the Jansenists, and Jesuits. Finally Arnold glances at Joubert's British contemporary, Lord Jeffrey; thence it is an easy step to Lord Macaulay, "the great apostle of the Philistines". Now, Macaulay was but a few years dead, and still an idol. Macaulay's future, Arnold thinks, will be brief, though now, as in his life, he enjoys fame and glory. The name of Joubert, on the other hand, scantly recognized as it is, and as it will be, will be handed down by the few to the few, an inextinguishable torch. At least Arnold here performs the service of rendering some of the really penetrating sayings of Joubert familiar to English readers. This is one of his most delightful and salutary essays.

There follows *Spinoza and the Bible*. I suppose it was Goethe who attracted Arnold to Spinoza, describing him as *ein Gottbetrunkener Mensch*. And George Eliot and others in England were also writing of him. But Spinoza was a congenial theme to Arnold, and he writes well of him.

The volume closes with an essay on *Marcus Aurelius*. Sir Edmund Chambers wishes that we might have had Arnold's work on Lucretius completed. I confess to misgivings. Lucretius saw the mischief in the Stoics' doctrine: they were at once the enemies of science, the enemies of curiosity of any intellectual kind, and, in general, crampers of the human spirit. Arnold's essentially faulty historic sense makes him represent the Spaniard, Marcus Aurelius, one of the last Stoics, as closely akin to the Victorian Age! It may be that a generation hence many willingly will turn to a creed like that of Marcus Aurelius: so rapidly are we slipping away into a world where neither will society have any common hope, nor the individual any scope or ambition or consciousness of worth. But this is not, it seems to me, one of the points on which Matthew Arnold was endowed with a gift of prophecy, as he was with regard to the deadening effects of American materialism. Here he misunderstood. He is sincere about Marcus Aurelius. We can see it both in his published references to him, and in his private notes. He undoubtedly found in the Roman Emperor's meditations a stay and fortification when himself overtaken by low spirits. We can have no quarrel with that. But he was wrong in obtruding these meditations into any high place in human thought. Neither Marcus Aurelius, nor any other Stoic, save only Cleanthes in his famous hymn, has any place in literature; none of them were philosophers; their creed was as ignoble, almost, as that of any of the dissenting sects whom Arnold despised; that such a barren reef should ever have gladdened the hearts of men is merely an indication of the immeasurable sea of misery which surrounded them.

Here then, in briefest outline, as it strikes at least one reader, three-quarters of a century afterwards, is Arnold's work, *Essays in Criticism* of 1865. Victoria had been on her throne nearly a generation. How unlike the usual notion of the Victorian Age is this book! How mocking and stinging, and un-self-centred and un-self-complacent! One may retort: "But Arnold was one in forty million Victorians, and an unpopular, caricatured figure!" Hardly so, in 1865. His fame had risen, and was still to rise; four years earlier he had risked his official career as adviser in matters of education,[3] and won; true he was not now, nor ever in his lifetime, popular, but he had won the respect of many circles. He had gathered the ground under his feet, as Huxley was presently to do, and as neither Carlyle nor Ruskin ever succeeded in doing, being sounder than either, and having a surer grasp of Truth; above all he had begun to teach intelligent men at least the elements of criticism, even though occasionally his own powers failed: criticism not merely of literature in the narrow sense—for Arnold literature had no narrow sense,—but in politics and social structure, and in religion and every yearning of the human spirit. In versatility and range, in acumen and

---

[3]By opposing the "Revised Code" of Mr. Lowe, later Lord Sherbrooke. The code would have saved State expenditure by abolishing many of the recent reforms in education.

profundity, in philosophic premise and practical application nothing of this sort had yet been seen in English criticism. I have pointed to a shortcoming which, so far as I know, has gone unnoticed, and I am willing to agree with others, that there may be a mis-statement or two, an example of journalistic style, some mistakes. Yet it is salutary for us all to remember the solid achievement of the book. Much of it is imperishable.

In 1867 Arnold delivered at Oxford some lectures on Celtic literature. It has been represented that he was at this time so confident and self-complacent a mentor to the whole British people that he was ready to talk about anything—even a subject of which he knew nothing, such as Celtic literature. Anyone who had read the current opinions of Arnold, rather than Arnold's own work, might think such statements true. Those who will take the trouble to read these lectures and the preface Arnold wrote when he published them, will see at a glance that such statements are a gross perversion of what Arnold did and said. He merely used the interest of the Welsh and Irish in their own native literatures as a peg on which to hang certain very suggestive criticisms of the monotonous outlook of English society, and of the ghastly mistakes the English were making in governing Ireland. Though he had Cornish blood in his veins Arnold never pretended to any knowledge of Celtic literature or history. He had no philological lore, as he had been ready to admit in his argument with Professor Newman. Only, as a curious and cultivated Englishman, he was interested in the annual gatherings where Welsh literature and music were recited and played. The Welsh were not interfered with in this matter, as were the Bretons in France. On the other hand the *Times* made such gatherings an occasion for fulminating against their "mischievous and selfish sentimentalism" and told Welshmen that the "intelligence and music of Europe had come mainly from Teutonic sources". In a similarly heavy-handed way Englishmen were wont to jeer at the Irish for their religion and everything else the Irish held dear. When Mr. Peel had suggested the purchase of valuable Irish manuscripts for the British Museum, Macaulay, a governor of the Museum, had vetoed it. Arnold mildly inquired whether this sort of attitude, this provincial and Philistine outlook of the English and Scotch, had anything to do with the chronic difficulty in governing Ireland. Proceeding on this basis he went on to inquire whether the Celts had perhaps, after all, left traces on their English conquerors, and contributed to their culture. Disclaiming any knowledge of his own, but quoting from others, he tried to give some specimens of Celtic genius to his audience, and ventured the suggestion that chairs of Celtic Literature be established in some of the British universities.

That is a very brief description of these lectures, but I am confident that no one who will read them can find them different in temper or scope from my description. Yet Saintsbury, and others following him, have said that by plunging into a department of literature of which he knew nothing, Arnold encouraged others to do the same, and so had a mischievous effect on English criticism! On the contrary, the lectures were an ironical political sermon, which had some good results. Here again Arnold had something of a prophet's outlook. Perhaps it is worth remarking that Goldwin Smith, who at this period usually bickered with his friend, Matthew Arnold, was later, after residence in the United States, to lament the American desire to "roll the world flat and paint it red".

In the same year, 1867, the *New Poems* appeared, and had a marked success.

In 1868 he lost his infant son, and also his eldest boy, who had always been an invalid.

In 1869 Arnold published *Culture and Anarchy*. This is sometimes represented as a new venture— an incursion into politics! Instead, it follows, in natural sequence, his previous development. Nor does the last chapter of *Culture and Anarchy* point forward to the books on religion any more than previous work has done.

To many *Culture and Anarchy* is Arnold's best known work. This I think unfortunate both for him and his readers. For despite its solid core it is neither so well thought out, nor so well written as much of his other work. It was a troubled time. Europe presented a confounding spectacle. Fenianism was giving the British authorities trouble both at home and in America. America itself was beginning its long innings of stark materialism, and this, which Arnold hated and most dreaded, was being held up by public men in England as an example to imitate. It was obvious to Arnold that European civilization was in the crucible. And of real statesmanship there seemed to be little or none in England. The extension of the franchise, 1867, was a mere trick of Disraeli to "dish the Whigs". Carlyle called it *Shooting Niagara*; only Arnold seemed to realize its implications in the way of State education. Most of the voices one heard were angry and strident. Arnold's own voice took on a strident tone. In *Culture and Anarchy*, excepting the chapter on *Sweetness and Light*, which was originally an Oxford lecture, and in *Friendship's Garland*, a series of letters to the *Pall Mall Gazette*, 1866-70, he is almost the journalist in style. There remains a certain urbanity, but he has nearly forsaken the ironic method of *Essays in Criticism*. The long involved sentences and the endless repetition resemble a type of popular oratory. And these pieces had the success of popular oratory; their phrases were soon in everyone's mouth, and indeed are still much used.

But there is a solid core. Arnold's doctrine on the State, in the chapter, *Doing as One Likes*, is worth notice. It is based on one of the most striking and durable of Greek achievements; their theory of *Nomos*, which may be translated *Law*, if we use the term in its most philosophic sense; alternately a self-imposed restraint on one's lower desires and momentary impulses, and a desire to give scope to one's best impulses; and yet never an individual affair, because civilized man never lives by himself, always in society, but a rule and law socially framed and socially adhered to. Now, such a conception is difficult, it even involves contradictions, as the Greeks themselves were well aware. For how can a man ever be said to rule himself, or to realize himself? And how can a man be both a free individual and yet a disciplined member of society? But then, as the Greeks knew, life is made up of differences, inconsistencies, contradictions. One aims at the greatest harmony possible; ἐκ τῶν διαφερόντων καλλίστη ἁρμονία said one of them. Not only is it one of the noblest social theories ever formulated: it has had since the time of Hugo de Groot a profound influence on the life and thought of Western Europe. Leonard Woolf in his savage criticism of Arnold's politics[4] makes no allusion to it. Arnold makes no attempt to elaborate the theory; he knows that scholars who may read him will follow a hint or two and expand it for themselves. But he strives valiantly to apply the theory, in a practical way, to the minds of contemporary Englishmen in general. In the first chapter he had quoted Montesquieu (who had expounded the Greek idea of Law to *his* countrymen): to "make an intelligent being more intelligent"; and his favourite author, Bishop Wilson: "to make reason and the will of God prevail"; and had shown that no individual could apply these rules to himself without at the same time striving to make the rule general in society. No man can be happy in an unhappy society. "The armies of the homeless and unfed" will not let him. Now, in the second chapter, Arnold tries to show that in England there is no real *society*. Classes, interests, sects, are each playing their own game, and every individual is clamouring, and with some success, for the maximum of personal liberty. As Arnold had been saying for many a day, Liberalism of the old type had accomplished its purpose, but could not meet the

[4] *After the Deluge.*

present situation. What was now needed was a public conscience. Now, not only was this phrase meaningless, he complained, to most of his contemporaries: the word, *conscience*,[5] itself had been limited to moral matters,—its application to intellectual and political matters was not so much denied as undreamed of. In proclaiming that the rule of the best self over the inferior self must be collectively applied, applied through a new conception of the State, Arnold was the inspiration of many who followed in British politics.

Once again, then, we see that to set a date on Arnold's writing helps us greatly to understand it. To read *Culture and Anarchy* by itself, or only with an editor's foot-notes, makes it a difficult, even a formidable book. Reading it after *Essays in Criticism*, and side by side with *Friendship's Garland*, that series of newspaper articles written during the portentous expansion of Prussia, one has many clues. Herbert Paul said of *Friendship's Garland*: "the fun is immortal, and the criticism deep as well as sound. . . . The charm of these pages, the most vivacious that even Mr. Arnold ever penned, lies in the inimitable drollness of the social satire." Then, after quoting more than two pages as a sample, he adds: "I do not think that Matthew Arnold ever surpassed this dialogue." Now, we may be pleased that Arnold

[5]See essay on Joubert.

collected these newspaper articles and republished them. They reveal the gaiety and high spirits upon which G. W. E. Russell and other personal friends have remarked, high spirits which he deliberately cultivated, as we know from the Note-Book, as an antidote to hypochondria. But this was Arnold's occasional side, not his abiding temper, as letters to the press were not his usual method of addressing the public. Nor was broad farcical humour native to him; his forte was delicate irony. I am inclined to believe that the Prussian wars, Fenianism, the riots in London and elsewhere, and the double bereavement he suffered in 1868, had something to do with the *forced* character of his writing during this period.

The years 1870-77 were mainly given up to theological study and writing. It is impossible to think them a special episode in his life. The evidence is conclusive that he had pondered these matters for decades, and at length, with some reluctance, resolved to deal with them. Nor does the evidence allow us to think, even for a moment, that he was a mere dabbler in this field. Having said that much I observe the restriction I placed upon myself at the outset, and say nothing further on this part of his work.

The writing of the period which followed, including the bulk of the *Mixed Essays*, published 1879, the poem *Westminster Abbey*, published 1882, the *Irish Essays and Others* of the same year, the *Lectures* given in the United States and Canada, 1883-84, and the *Essays* which he collected just before his death,—all this rich and varied work seems to me to have a distinct character. There is no falling away in power, no less gracious a poetic inspiration on the single occasion when it occurs, nor is the cutting edge of his mind any less keen, whether in criticizing literature or politics, or schools, but there is a ripeness and mellowness, a serenity in his writing, that is hardly to be found before. In his private writings,—the letters from America, on both visits, and the slight but winsome poems on the loss of household pets,—it is distinctly observable. In the last years of his life Arnold was a happy man.

I have long thought that Arnold had one of the most positive and constructive political minds among modern Englishmen. He thought himself that he had an exceedingly, but not hopelessly, intractable material to deal with. He was conscious, in an amused way, of his affinity with Socrates in this respect. It is, indeed, difficult to talk to men of a thing into which they have never been initiated, of which they have no experience. What Arnold desiderated in English public life was an intelligence that could grasp the great changes which were being forced on the age, almost from without, and a long-headed and not too selfish view of the future. But Englishmen, both at home and in the colonies, and Americans too, were thoughtlessly and selfishly living in the present: their philosophy, so-called, was that of "muddling through"; they were incapable of climbing the "specular mount" because the education which the bulk of the community gave themselves and their children was the worst in the world, and they persisted in this abominable education because they had never climbed the "specular mount". Arnold has tersely stated his creed in the essay, *The Future of Liberalism*: "Cobbett's politics were at bottom always governed by one master-thought—the evil condition of the English labourer,—the master-thought by which my politics are governed is rather this, the thought of the bad civilisation of the English middle class." At the end of the previous century Burke had lamented that Englishmen never willingly gave attention to the plight of Ireland: only external dangers could coerce them to do so. Arnold sincerely and prophetically feared that there would be no imaginative statesmanship either about Ireland or about education until it was too late. Well, we know the sequel! Arnold's writing about Ireland is inspired, it is work of sheer genius. Here at least there was no lack of an adequate historic sense. He told the English that they must not only *act differently* in Ireland, they must *be different*; and he traced in an ample, impartial way their attitude to the Irish since the Plantagenet Conquest; and more particularly since the Tudors. In 1913 a visitor to Belfast, headquarters of the Northcliffe Rebellion, to Dublin, seething with the Larkin riots, and to remoter parts of Ireland, heard, when he encountered English observers of the tumultuous scene, various panaceas, some of them as stupid as Balfour's "twenty years of resolute government", but none of them imaginative, few of them even based on history. The visitor found himself thinking of *Utopia*, the political writing of one of the gentlest souls in the sixteenth century, but a mere Englishman when he touched on Ireland. More exhorted his readers to exterminate the Irish. The deadly mischief lay in this: that the Irish came to know this English attitude, and, though one accident and another prevented the consummation of the policy, the Irish remnant were never grateful for the accidents. In the scenes which could be observed in 1913, a recollection of Arnold's *Irish Essays*, rather than of Burke, or Swift, or Mrs. J. R. Green, made one distrust the glib panaceas at least, and made one wonder whether Fate had been more malign to the stricken Irish or to their impotent conquerors.

What Arnold said of schools fell on ears nearly as deaf. Indeed it was not until twenty-eight years after his death, and when beset by perils undreamed of hitherto, that the British Government seriously began to consider education as one of its own activities. Though the Fisher Act, of 1918, to which this consideration led, was soon whittled down, we can still say that, since the War, there have been vast and far-reaching reforms in English primary and secondary schools. It is still true that the bulk of the children of well-to-do parents are sent to expensive private schools. In few particulars has Arnold's advice been followed. But the spirit of his doctrine has at last leavened the minds of Englishmen: they are at last seriously in earnest about education. American writers have complained that in their country, long, long before Arnold's visits, the State had taken over not only primary and secondary but even university education, and that Arnold gave them no credit for it. What Arnold missed, as he wrote to an American friend, was intellectual quality in any part of the American scheme. Their colleges were "pullulating", but what did that amount to? On this continent, and in this country, we have still nearly all Arnold's teaching to apply in the matter of education. Not even our universities would stand Arnold's question: "Do you aim at giving a taste for the best that has been known and thought in the world?" As for our secondary schools they are full of jargon about economics, political science, and civics, crowded with a multiplicity of subjects, deadened by the memorizing of text-books and preparation for competitive examinations which Mahaffy, and Arnold with him, deplored in the schools of Ireland. It is at least debatable whether Canadian schools have not gone backward, instead of forward, in the past quarter century.

Soon after they appeared, bound together in one volume, 1908, I bought and read Arnold's *Mixed Essays* and *Irish Essays*, first published separately, 1879 and 1882. Few modern books I know have stood re-reading over thirty years as this book has done. That by the way. But I have sometimes wished, in the last troubled years, that all who have to do with our public affairs, all who undertake to write and edit our newspapers, all who have to do in an official way with our schools, could be somehow induced to read and study at least that much of Matthew Arnold. True, it contains some purely literary essays: *A French Critic on Milton*, *A French Critic on Goethe*, the exquisite essay on George Sand, at which few such Canadians would do more than glance. But they might be attracted by other titles: *Democracy*, *Equality*; or by some accident be led into the *Irish Essays*, and from that point I am sure they would go on. There is so much profound knowledge of the heart of man here;

such a large and winning urbanity; such a sweet reasonableness. One sees, too, almost at first blush, how prophetic this writing has been. It has been one of the greatest pleasures of my life that I have been able of recent years to distribute what I call *germinal* books in school libraries, and in other places where I know they will be read. But these essays of Arnold, alas! whether in one volume or two, are out of print, and hard to secure even second-hand. Before I pass on from this collection let me add that the essay on George Sand gives, I think, more than any other single prose piece, an insight into Arnold's own mind.

To come to the prose of his last years. First, the preface to the collection of Johnson's *Lives of the Poets*. Here, as a pleasant gesture to Macaulay's shade, Arnold included his *Life of Johnson*, saying with truth that this was Macaulay at his best. In the preface Arnold deals concisely with our eighteenth-century literature. Is it not almost the final word? One who has lived through, in Oxford and elsewhere, the valiant attempt to whittle down the edge of Arnold's judgment, who has seen attempts even to reverse that judgment, especially on Pope, sees at length that the verdict stands. In the same year Arnold wrote an introduction to his selection of Wordsworth's poems. This essay has often been singled out for praise. A Wordsworthian from youth, Arnold is yet detached enough to reject most of Wordsworth's work. And the wisdom of his selection seems to be more and more approved. In 1880 Arnold wrote *The Study of Poetry* as an introduction to Ward's collection of English poetry. This collection fell into my hands in school-days. The preface was the first of Arnold's criticism I had encountered. Much of it was above me. But what a doorway for a lad so under the spell of the *Iliad* as to wonder whether he was under a trance of his own, or whether Homer affected all readers so, to read that the love of great poetry is the highest of all experiences, and to find that, of eleven passages cited to illustrate great poetry, three were from the beloved *Iliad*! Of that enough. Here we should observe that these three prefaces mentioned, and the essays on Gray and Keats of the same time, have a freshness and joy about them, as though Arnold, turning from theology, with a sigh like that of Faust,[6] were rediscovering old pleasures.

Arnold is usually thought to have rated Keats too low. If so, this appears in such places as the essay on Byron, where by implication Keats is ruled out. But in the essay on Keats, as in the reference to him in the Homer lectures, twenty years earlier, surely the praise is very high. Keats in more than one place is ranked with

---
[6]*Und leider auch Theologie!*

Shakespeare, or only below Shakespeare. Not only is there great discernment into Keats' work and his own self-criticism: when Arnold begins to speak of his "magic" we see that he has fallen under Keats' peculiar spell, that he is intoxicated with the loveliness and felicity of Keats, and with that poet's own intoxication with Beauty.

When one is young, and lost in admiration of Shelley, as all young people ought to be, Arnold's judgment of him seems unsympathetic and perverse. Arnold planned to write again of Shelley; in the review of Dowden's life, which we have, he expressly says he writes only of Shelley's character. As a character study it is not unsympathetic. Nor is his condemnation of Shelley's poetry wholly condemnatory: "beautiful and ineffectual angel, beating in the void his luminous wings in vain", he called him in the essay on Byron. But the youthful admirer of a passage like:

> I stand at noon upon the peak of Heaven,
> Then with unwilling steps I wander down
> Into the clouds of the Atlantic even:
> For grief that I depart they weep and frown.
> What look is more delightful than the smile
> With which I greet them from the western isle?

—the admirer of a passage like this will exclaim: "Why must the angel's wings be effective as well as luminous? Is the critic not paying too much heed to Shelley's own disclaimer, 'You might as well go to a gin-shop for a leg of mutton as expect anything earthly or human from me'?" Later, I do not know just why, we find ourselves admitting that perhaps Shelley "stands on the back of the sky" too much, and correspondingly Arnold's criticism affronts us less. Even the startling judgment that perhaps Shelley will live longer by his letters and prose than by his poetry, though it was a rash saying, we begin to find has at least this basis: that whereas Shelley's poetry is addressed to our youth, and at best seems youthful, his prose is the work of a mature man and addressed to our maturity.

It is Arnold's judgment about Byron that baffles our maturity. There was a time when most of us felt as he feels about Byron. But what led Arnold, delivering a final judgment, when he was nearly sixty, to overrate Byron so? True, Goethe had rated him high, the Germans in this century were still calling him our greatest modern poet, and other continental writers have done the same. And, from Arnold's point of view Byron had hated the right things, the selfish aristocrats, the Puritans and Philistines. Or was it a lack of impetuosity in Arnold's own muse that made him admire so and almost envy the headstrong inspiration of Byron—"Byron's force" he called it in the early poem? Had we best say of Arnold, as Arnold said of Johnson, that we must not take it amiss if he fails us here and there? Let Arnold's detractors make the most of his judgment on Byron, they will hardly find in him such another lapse!

In contrast with this, let us look at a literary criticism Arnold wrote at the very end of his life, almost, the *Essay on Tolstoi*. It is said nowadays that Arnold missed fire in criticizing contemporaries, that he only showed well in writing of authors who had already been discussed hundreds or thousands of years. Well, I know hardly anything better on Tolstoi than this essay. And Arnold might easily have gone widely wrong here. Hardly anything was yet known in Western Europe of Russian literature. It is obvious that Arnold himself had never heard of Pushkin or Aksakov. And *Anna Karenina* might at first sight appear a sprawling work to so disciplined a mind as Arnold's. But sheer genius stands out in it, and Arnold not only recognizes it but points unerringly to the qualities that make it up: sensitiveness to human experience; delicacy of insight into the human heart; the power of depicting tragedy so as to make it beautiful, pleasurable, and a moral refreshment; marvellous power in portraying character.

I say nothing of the three essays which Arnold used as his lectures in America, not because they are in any way negligible, but to have space to call attention to an essay on the United States, which will now, I am confident, become better known because it has been included, with just the right comment, in the excellent selection of prose work recently made by Professor E. K. Brown.[7] I am almost certain it is the last thing Arnold wrote; at any rate it appeared in the month in which he died, and hence is a fitting thing with which to conclude. I observe that Professor Brown sets it as a sort of climax to his selection. It exhibits so many of Arnold's characteristics: his courage in facing the Truth, and yet his skill in winding into it—he had not read Plato for nothing; his sympathetic humanity—has any more graceful tribute been paid to the peculiar charm of American women?—his power to grapple with the heart of a subject; his sheer mental strength in seeing things as they really are, and with a backward and forward look. Finally it is a masterpiece of Greek irony: what he says of abundance of ice, and of fruit for breakfast, the most illiterate American or Canadian understands, up to a point; Europeans will understand it in another context; a reader of culture and wisdom catches the deep meaning, as well as the overtones.

[7]*Representative Essays of Matthew Arnold*, Toronto, Macmillan, 1936.

INDEX

Academy, the French, 130
Aeschylus, 36, 62
Alaric at Rome, 18
Alcman, 95
Alexandria, 65, 91
Aristophanes, 68, 100
Aristotle, 89, 113, 120
Arnold, Matthew
    character of his age, 13-16
    his relation to his age, 16 *ff*., 33-4, 60, 125, 136, 145 *ff*.
    interest in politics, social questions, 18 *ff*.
    interest in religion, 18, 28, 71, 99
    appreciation of science, 30, 31
    lack of historic sense, 29, 69, 132, 135
    health, 27, 28
    personality, 25 *ff*., 44
    marriage, 46, 75
    bereavements, 90, 139
    Arnold and his father, 76-7
    influence of Greek literature on, 38-40
    Arnold and Middle Ages, 72, 74
    his learning, 123-4
    school inspector, 52, 99 *et passim*
    poetic genius of, 39, 41 *ff*., 66-8, 88-98, 122-3
    his prose, 40, 61, 100, 105, 113, 140-1, 144
    critical power, 31 *ff*., 112, 114, 117-19, 120-1, 136-7, 150, 153, 154
    largely out of print, 16, 99
    present reputation, 16-17
    errors of his critics through ignorance of chronology, 64, 88, 100-3, 123
    happy in his last years, 145
Arnold, Dr. Thomas, 25, 28, 76-7

Bacchanalia, 51, 80
Bagehot, Walter, 29
Balder Dead, 36, 39, 68-9, 91, 115
Brown, E. K., 155
Browning, Robert, 38, 56, 60, 69, 89, 114
Budd, William, M.D., 23, 24

INDEX

The Buried Life, 57, 94
Burke, Edmund, 127, 128, 146, 147
Butler, Samuel, 46
Byron, 59, 153-4

Canada, 145, 149
Carlyle, Thomas, 31, 77, 136, 140
Celtic literature, 137-9
Chamberlain, Joseph, 77
Chambers, Sir Edmund, 16, 17, 47, 134
Chartists, 20
Child labour, 20-2, 39
Clapham, J. A., 19, 21, 22
Cleanthes, 135
Clough, A. H., 18, 27, 28, 44, 46, 47, 48, 60, 64, 65-7, 88, 90, 102, 103-5, 122
Cobbett, 23, 146
Coleridge, 111
Consolation, 62
Cowper, 116
Culture and Anarchy, 124, 139-44

Dante, 35, 36, 117, 119
Darwin, Charles, 31, 77
Deceased Wife's Sister Bill, 48
de Guérin, 130-1
de Senancour, 58
Dickens, 91
Dissenters, 28, 29, 30
Doing As One Likes, 141
Dover Beach, 74-5, 83, 114
A Dream, 47, 57

Eliot, George, 17
Eliot, T. S., 17, 91
Elizabethan tragedy, 38
Emerson, 42
Empedocles, 50, 53
Empedocles on Etna, 52, 53, 54, 55, 56, 58, 59, 60, 61, 62, 81, 93, 113, 114
Epidemics, 23, 24
Epilogue to Lessing's Laocoön, 91

INDEX 159

Essays in Criticism (1865), 122-37, 141, 143
Euripides, 38

Faded Leaves, 47, 49
Forsaken Merman, 43, 44, 45, 47, 48, 49, 60, 92-3, 98
Friendship's Garland, 140, 143-4
Froude, J. A., 24, 43, 44, 45, 60
Function of Criticism at the Present Time, 125-9
The Future, 59, 94

Garrod, Professor H. W., 47
Gladstone, 101, 125
God and the Bible, 84
Goethe, 58, 89, 95, 109, 128
Gray, 53, 54, 89, 151
Greece, and the Greeks, 15, 32, 33, 34, 35, 37, 38, 39, 53, 54, 63, 65, 74, 88-91, 95, 100, 103, 108-9, 110-11, 112, 133, 140-1
Green, Mrs. J. R., 147
Grotius, (Hugo de Groot), 142

Hardy, Thomas, 38
Heine, 131-2
Herodotus, 41, 42, 43, 65, 77
Homer, 18, 35, 36, 37, 41, 50, 61, 62, 65, 68, 69, 77, 86, 88, 115-20, 151
Housman, A. E., 117-18
Huxley, Thomas, 31, 77, 136

Iliad, 61, 151
Irish Essays, 145-50
Irish immigrants, 19-20
Irish Question, 31, 32, 137-8, 145-50

Johnson, Samuel, 150
Joubert, 133-4
Journalism, 140-1, 143-4

Keats, 56, 59, 110, 151-2
Krumbacher, Karl, 38

Landor, 89
Lang, Andrew, 79-80

INDEX

Lansdowne, Lord (3rd Marquess, 1780-1863), 102
The Last Word, 98, 114
Law, Greek conception of, 141
Legouis, M., 46
Letters (M. Arnold's, ed. by Russell), 25, 101
    Russell's preface mentioned, 144
Letters (to Clough), 46
Liberalism, 142, 146
Literature and Dogma, 84
Lowe, Robert, Lord Sherbrooke, 136
Lowry, Professor H. F., 46, 47, 66, 102-3, 105
Lucretius, 36, 50, 53, 54, 82, 89, 134

Macaulay, T. B., 31, 112, 113, 134, 138, 150
Machiavelli, 33
Marcus Aurelius, 134-5
Margaret, Marguerite, 45, 46, 47, 48, 49, 52, 56, 58, 68, 82, 114
Memory Picture, 47, 48
Merope, 39, 69-70, 91, 115
Mills, the two, 77
Milton, 35, 36, 38, 42, 51, 62, 63, 67-8, 70, 79, 88, 102, 117
Mixed Essays, 144-50
Montesquieu, 142
Morality, 55, 59
More, Sir Thomas, 147
Morley, John, 77
Morris, William, 56
Mycerinus, 42, 43, 50, 59, 92, 98, 102

Neckan, 44
Newman, J. H., 18, 31
Newman, Professor, 116-17
New Sirens, 47, 48, 52, 60
Norse (mythology), 68-9

Obermann, 53, 57, 58
Obermann Once More, 80-3, 98, 114
On the Rhine, 49
On Translating Homer, 115-20, 122, 123
Oxford, 18, 28, 31, 64, 90, 115, 126, 137

Pagan and Mediaeval Religious Sentiment, 132-3
Parmenides, 53
Parting, 45, 48
Paul, Herbert, 101, 113, 143
Peel, Robert, 138
Philistine, 132, 138, 153
Pindar, 53
Plato, 32, 33, 37, 42, 53, 67-8, 89, 155
Pope, Alexander, 150
Preface of 1853, 106-15, 120, 123
Preface to *Essays in Criticism* (1865), 126
Progress, 59
Puritans, 33, 77, 153

Resignation, 49, 50, 51, 52, 58, 62, 74, 93, 99, 105, 114
Rubens, 33
Rugby Chapel, 95-7, 98, 114
Ruskin, John, 31, 77, 116, 136

St. Brandan, 56, 57
St. Paul and Protestantism, 57, 84
Sainte-Beuve, 103, 130
Saintsbury, 43, 101
Sand, George, 102, 130, 149-50
Scholar Gipsy, 51, 60, 62, 64-7, 80, 94, 97, 114
Schools, 22, 23, 25, 32, 99, 100, 115, 146-9
Self-Dependence, 55, 59
Separation, 68
Shakespeare, 66, 68, 109, 110, 112
Shakespeare (Sonnet), 24, 42, 78, 101
Shelley, 37, 38, 51, 68, 152-3
Sidney, Philip, 68
Smith, Goldwin, 60, 139
Smith, Logan Pearsall, 124
Snow, John, M.D., 23
Socrates, 16
Sohrab and Rustum, 36, 60, 61-4, 66, 78, 94, 98, 123
Sonnets to a Friend, 18, 41, 42
Sophocles, 18, 43, 68, 77
A Southern Night, 115
Spenser, 37

Spinoza, 134
Stanley, Arthur, 84-6, 88
Stanzas from the Grande Chartreuse, 71-4, 114
Stephen, Fitzjames, 76
Stoics, 75, 134-5
Strachey, Lytton, 103
A Strayed Reveller, 41, 62
Strew on her Roses, Roses, 68
Study of Poetry, 151
Summer Night, 55
Sweetness and Light, 140
Swift, 147
Swinburne, A. C., 38, 60, 67, 81
Switzerland, 46, 71, 81, 94, 115
Switzerland, 46, 47, 48

Teniers, 33
Tennyson, 16, 36, 37, 43, 56, 59, 60, 84, 97, 102, 116-17
Terrace at Berne, 46
Theocritus, 51, 53, 64, 88, 133
Theology, 25, 144
Theophrastus, 15
Thucydides, 77, 121
Thyrsis, 43, 51, 78-80, 88, 94, 98, 102, 114, 122
Tolstoi, 154
To Marguerite (Yes! in the Sea of Life), 48, 92, 115
Tristram and Iseult, 47, 56, 72, 93, 97
Trollope, Mrs., 91
Tyndall, John, 30, 31

United States, 32, 135, 139, 140, 145, 155

Vergil, 35, 36, 95, 117, 119
Verses from the Carnac, 115
The Voice, 47, 48, 52

Wales, 137-8
Westminster Abbey, 84-8, 144
Wightman, Miss, 46
Wilson, Bishop, 142
A Wish, 95-7

INDEX

Woolf, Leonard (*After the Deluge*), 142
Wordsworth, 42, 46, 49, 50, 57, 58, 59, 67, 89, 93, 94, 111, 150-1

Yes! in the Sea of Life (To Marguerite), 48, 92, 115
Young, G. M., 23
The Youth of Man, 59
The Youth of Nature, 59, 66

www.ingramcontent.com/pod-product-compliance
Lightning Source LLC
Chambersburg PA
CBHW020417080526
44584CB00014B/1369